HINDUSTANI GRAMMAR SELF-TAUGHT

HINDUSTANI GRAMMAR SELF-TAUGHT

IN FOUR PARTS :—

I. A SIMPLIFIED GRAMMAR.
II. EXERCISES AND EXAMINATION PAPERS.
III. THE VERNACULAR.
IV. KEY AND ENGLISH-HINDUSTANI DICTIONARY

BY

CAPT. C. A. THIMM.

SHAMS'UL 'ULAMA SAYYID 'ALI BILGRAMI,

M. A. Cantab., LL.B., Assoc. R.S.M., London, M.R.A.S.

GYAN

Published by

GYAN

Gyan Publishing House
5, Ansari Road
Daryaganj, New Delhi-110002
Phone: 011-47034999, 9811692060
E-mail: books@gyanbooks.com

Distribution Network
gyanbooks.com
India, USA, Canada, UK, Australia, France

ISBN : 978-81-212-4425-1 (PB)
First Published, 1916

2nd Impression 2020

Printed at: Gyan Press, Delhi.

Hindustani Grammar
Self-Taught
Author: Capt. C. A. thimm

Hindūstāni Grammar Self-Taught.

In Four Parts :—

I. A Simplified Grammar.
II. Exercises and Examination Papers.
III. The Vernacular.
IV. Key and English-Hindustani Dictionary.

By Capt. C. A. THIMM.

Third Edition. Revised by

SHAMS'UL 'ULAMĀ SAYYID 'ALI BILGRĀMĪ,

M.A. Cantab., LL.B., Assoc. R.S.M., London, M.R.A.S.

E. Marlborough & Co., 51, Old Bailey, London, E.C.
1916.

PREFACE TO SECOND EDITION.

The first edition of this work being exhausted, in view of the many evidences of its usefulness which have been received, the Publishers decided to adopt some of the suggestions made to further increase the practical usefulness and reliability of the book, and placed the work in the hands of SHAMS'UL 'ULAMA SAYYID 'ALI BILGRAMI, M.A., M.R.A.S., etc., who undertook the necessary revision.

Owing to the unfortunate and serious illness of Mr. BILGRAMI during the progress of the work, however, Mr. J. F. BLUMHARDT, M.A., M.R.A.S., very kindly consented to see the new edition through the Press, and the Publishers are greatly indebted to him for his courtesy and care in passing the proofs, thus bringing the work to a satisfactory conclusion.

The volume has therefore had the advantage of an entire revision, many valuable suggestions have been embodied, involving the re-writing of several pages, and new matter of a useful character has been added, including the numerals on pp. 42-43 and an extra page of sentences in English and Hindūstānī, with the romanized form, on p. 81.

The practical value and importance of the volume have been greatly enhanced, and students will find it exceedingly useful as an introduction to the study of the Hindūstānī language.

London, 1907.

PREFACE.

DURING the compilation of "Hindūstānī Self-Taught"* it became apparent that a second volume would be needed by those who require more than a passing knowledge of the language, and especially by those preparing for the Government Examinations, to provide them with the essential points and rules of Grammar in a simplified form.

The Hindūstānī Exercises, with notes to illustrate the construction of the language, are mainly founded on words and phrases in "Hindūstānī Self-Taught," and the *ad literatim* English interlinear translation is given to show at a glance the difference of idiom between the two languages, especially for those who have not the advantage of a teacher.

A translation into Hindūstānī of MR. RUDYARD KIPLING'S poem, "SHIV AND THE GRASSHOPPER,"† has been made by special permission of the author, and I heartily acknowledge the kind way in which MR. KIPLING consented to the use of his poem.

"THE LORD'S PRAYER," also rendered into Hindūstānī, has the *Phonetic Pronunciation* given, which may perhaps prove useful to some, as well as serve the educational purposes of the book.

Romanized characters have been mainly used, but those who desire to carry their studies further will find in Section III. a valuable introduction to the Persi-Arabic characters. Added to which, sets of Examination Papers are given, with full Key at end.

My best thanks are due to Don M. de Zilva Wickremasinghe, of the Indian Institute at Oxford, and to Maulavie Mohammad Barakatullah, The Oriental Academy, 124, Chancery Lane, W.C., for the valuable suggestions and corrections made in the work by them.

It is earnestly hoped that these books may prove of some little service in binding the great Empire of India still closer to the British Nation, and that many whose duty or pleasure calls them to India may find their way made easier and more effective through their possession.

Any suggestions that may enhance their usefulness will be gladly received by the publishers in London.

---

* THIMM (C. A.) Hindūstānī Self-Taught. [In Romanized characters.] Containing Vocabularies, Idiomatic Phrases and Dialogues, Travel Talk, Military, Legal, Religious, Commercial, Shooting and Fishing Terms, Money, Weights and Measures, Indian Titles Castes, Festivals, &c., &c. Crown 8vo., wrapper, Do., do., bound in cloth, E. MARLBOROUGH & CO., 51, Old Bailey, London, E.C.

† The Jungle Book (pages 244 and 245). By Rudyard Kipling. (1900. London: Macmillan & Co., Ltd.)

CONTENTS.

PART I.

THE ALPHABET, RULES OF GRAMMAR, AND PARTS OF SPEECH.

(Pages 6–43.)

PART II.

EXERCISES AND EXAMINATION PAPERS.

(Pages 44-72.)

PART III.

THE VERNACULAR.

(Pages 73–86.)

PART IV.

KEY AND DICTIONARY.

(Pages 87–120.)

HINDŪSTĀNĪ GRAMMAR.

PART I.

THE ALPHABET, RULES OF GRAMMAR, AND PARTS OF SPEECH.

Hindūstānī, or Urdū,* is the language most widely spoken in India. The Mahomedan population throughout the Empire generally use it, and it is the recognised native official language of the country.

Strictly speaking, it is an important form of Hindi; but, whereas the latter is always written in the Deva-nāgarī (Sanskrit) characters, Hindūstānī is written mainly in the Persi-Arabic characters. Indeed, the peculiarity of the language is the large admixture of Persian and Arabic words originating from the official and daily intercourse of the Persian-speaking rulers with their Hindu subjects after the great Mahomedan conquest of India. So that we

---

* "Urdū" is the native term for the language, and is originally a Persian word signifying "a camp."

find, while the Urdū, or *Rekhta*, abounds with words and phrases from the Persian and Arabic languages, the Hindī consists of words of native origin or words borrowed from the Sanskrit.

The purest form of the tongue is spoken only in the North-West Provinces; but it has really developed into a kind of *lingua vulga* for the whole of India, and even in the South a more or less corrupted form of it is spoken, known as *Dakhanī*.

Since both Persian and Arabic employ a script derived from the Semitic stock, the Urdū characters (printed or written) are read from *right* to *left*. This adds to their somewhat bewildering effect on the mind of a student beginning to learn the language, but with a little patient perseverance in copying each letter with care over and over again, until it is familiarised to the eye and fixed in the memory, it is surprising how soon this initial difficulty may be overcome.

The main thing for the learner to remember is not to attempt too much at a time, two or three letters only being practised together, so that the mind clearly grasps and retains each individual character before proceeding to the next. This will save much time afterwards, and make all the future work more sure and easy.

The Alphabet consists of 35 letters. Of these, 28 are primarily derived from the Arabic, 4 from the Persian, and 3 from the Devanāgarī or Sanskrit, and together they constitute the whole of the characters used in Hindūstānī.

The following tables show these in their various forms, with the Romanized equivalent so widely adopted at the present day.

THE ALPHABET IN PERSI-ARABIC
WITH ROMAN CHARACTERS.

Name.	Detached Form.	Forms used in Combination.			Roman Characters.
		Final.	Medial.	Initial.	
Alif	ا	ـا	ـا	ا	a (see p. 12)
Be	ب	ـب	ـبـ	بـ	b
Pe	پ	ـپ	ـپـ	پـ	p
Te	ت	ـت	ـتـ	تـ	t
Ṭa	ٹ	ـٹ	ـٹـ	ٹـ	ṭ
Ṣe	ث	ـث	ـثـ	ثـ	ṣ
Jīm	ج	ـج	ـجـ	جـ	j
Che	چ	ـچ	ـچـ	چـ	ch
Ḥe	ح	ـح	ـحـ	حـ	ḥ
K͟he	خ	ـخ	ـخـ	خـ	k͟h
Dāl	د	ـد	ـد	د	d
Ḍa	ڈ	ـڈ	ـڈ	ڈ	ḍ
Ẕāl	ذ	ـذ	ـذ	ذ	ẕ
Re	ر	ـر	ـر	ر	r
Ṛa	ڑ	ـڑ	ـڑ	ڑ	ṛ
Ze	ز	ـز	ـز	ز	z
Zhe	ژ	ـژ	ـژ	ژ	zh

Name.	Detached Form.	Forms used in Combination.			Roman Characters.
		Final.	Medial.	Initial.	
Sīn	س	ـس	ـسـ	سـ	s
Shīn	ش	ـش	ـشـ	شـ	sh
Ṣād	ص	ـص	ـصـ	صـ	ṣ
Ẓād	ض	ـض	ـضـ	ضـ	ẓ
T̤o,e	ط	ـط	ـطـ	طـ	t̤
Z̤o,e	ظ	ـظ	ـظـ	ظـ	z̤
'Ain	ع	ـع	ـعـ	عـ	' [1]
<u>Gh</u>ain	غ	ـغ	ـغـ	غـ	<u>gh</u>
Fe	ف	ـف	ـفـ	فـ	f
Ḳāf	ق	ـق	ـقـ	قـ	ḳ
Kāf	ک	ـک	ـکـ	کـ	k
Gāf	گ	ـگ	ـگـ	گـ	g
Lām	ل	ـل	ـلـ	لـ	l
Mīm	م	ـم	ـمـ	مـ	m
Nūn	ن	ـن	ـنـ	نـ	n [2]
Wā,o	و	ـو	ـو	و	w, o, u
He	ہ	ـہ	ـہـ ـھـ [3]	ہـ	h
Ye	ی	ـی	ـیـ	یـ	y, e, i

[1] A strong guttural breathing; no European equivalent.

[2] The form ں (ṇ) is used as a final nasal, see page 74.

[3] This form is used to aspirate a consonant.

Romanized Characters with Pronunciation.

Romanized Characters.	Pronunciation.
a	Resembles the English *u* in *up*, and sometimes *a* in *sat*.
ā, *ā̦*	As *a* long in *father*.
ai	Like *i* in *bite*, or *y* in *my*.
au	Like the English *ou* in *our*.
b	As *b* in *babble*.
bh	As *b* with aspiration, closely sounded together.
ch	Always the *soft* sound, as *ch* in *lurch*.
chh	As *ch* with aspiration, closely sounded together.
d	Very nearly as *d* in *dew;* uttered by applying point of tongue to roots of upper front teeth.
dh	As the *d* above, with aspiration closely sounded.
ḍ	Nearly like *d* in *dull;* uttered by striking point of tongue on palate.
ḍh	As the *d* above, with aspiration closely sounded, as *dh* in *woodhouse*.
e	As *ai* in *pair*, or *ay* in *pay*.
f	As *f* in *fill*.
g	As *g* in *good*.
gh	As *g* with aspiration, closely sounded together.
g͟h	A peculiar guttural sound, like that made in gargling.
h	As *h* in *horse*, but it serves to aspirate consonants, such as *b*, *ch*, *d*, *g*, *k*, *p*, &c., which see.
ḥ	As *h* forcibly expressed.
i	As *i* in *fit*.
ī	As *ee* in *feel*.
j	As *j* in *judge*.
jh	As *j* with aspiration, closely sounded together.
k	As *k* in *king*.
kh	As *k* with aspiration, closely sounded together, like *kh* in *workhouse*.
k͟h	Gutturally sounded with tremulous motion of throat, like *ch* in *loch*.
ḳ	As *k;* uttered by pressing back the root of the tongue on the throat, and making a slight clicking sound.
l, *m*, *n*	As in English.

Romanized Characters.	Pronunciation.
ṇ	A slight nasal sound, stronger than in the French "*bon.*"
n	As *n* sounded with tip of tongue on palate.
o	As *o* in *bone.*
p	As in English.
ph	As *p* with aspiration, closely sounded together.
r	As in English, but with more vibration.
ṛ	As double *r* (*rr*), sounded by striking tip of tongue on palate.
s	As *s* in *sin.*
sh	As *sh* in *shine.*
ṣ	As *s* in *us* by the people of India.
s̤	As *ṣ* above, but as pronounced by the Arabs it resembles *th* as in *thin.*
t, *t̤*	As in *tube* nearly, uttered with point of tongue on roots of upper teeth.
th	As *t* above, with aspiration, closely sounded together.
ṭ	As *t* in *tub* nearly.
ṭh	Aspirated *ṭ* like *th* in *Lofthouse.*
u	*Short*, as *u* in *pull, full.*
ū	*Long*, as *oo* in *cool.*
v	As in English.
w, *w̤**	Between *v* and *w*; when at end of word sound as *o*.
y	As in English.
z, *ẕ*, *ẓ*, *z̤*	As *z* in English without distinction by the people of India and Persia.
zh	As the French *j*, or *s* in *pleasure.*

The Romanized characters are used for the Hindūstānī words throughout.

* A hardly audible *w*, occurring in a few Persian words.

Vowels, Diphthongs, and Diacritical Marks.

The uses of vowels, diacritical marks, and their combinations call for careful notice.

There are *three Short* and *three Long* vowels.

The three Short Vowels *(initial or detached)* are :—

اَ (*a*) اِ (*i*) اُ (*u*)

The three Long Vowels are :—

آ (*ā*) اِي (*ī*) اُو (*ū*)

The diacritical signs when applied to vowels are placed above or below the letter affected thereby, as shown in above tables, and explained on page 13.

The Diphthongs, initial or detached, are :—

اي (*e*) اَي (*ai*) او (*o*) اَو (*au*)

The above vowels, when *combined with consonants*, are represented as follows :—

(Read from Right to Left.)

پَو	پو	پَي	پي	پُو	پُ	پِي	پِ	پَا	پَ
pau	*po*	*pai*	*pe*	*pū*	*pu*	*pī*	*pi*	*pā*	*pa*

اَور	اوك	اَيسا	ايك	اُود	اُس	اِيكھ	اِس	آس	اب
aur	*ok*	*aisā*	*ek*	*ūd*	*us*	*īkh*	*is*	*ās*	*ab*

It will be noticed that the vowels and diphthongs are formed by the three letters *Alif*, *Wāo*, and *Ye*—hence it follows that when not used as such they are consonants. All difficulties will disappear if it be borne in mind that they are consonants when initial in a word or syllable, in which case *Alif* is a kind of *spiritus lenis* (or soft breathing sound), and has the sign ء (*Hamza*) placed above it, particularly in words derived from Arabic.

With regard to the DIACRITICAL MARKS it will also be noticed that *three* are used in conjunction with *Alif* (ا), *Ye* (ي), and *Wāo* (و) to form combinations with consonants.

When so used these letters are known respectively as:

Fatḥa (َ),* the short *a* written above: thus,	بَد	bad
Kasra (ِ), ,, ,, *i* ,, below: ,,	دِن	din
Ẓamma (ُ), ,, ,, *u* ,, above: ,,	بُت	but

In addition to the above, there are *six* other diacritical signs; *three* applicable to vowels, and *three* applicable to consonants in words from the Arabic only.

The VOWEL SIGNS are used as under:—

(1) *Hamza* (ء), the *spiritus lenis* applied to the initial vowel, and is written thus:	جرأت	jur'at
(2) *Madda* (آ), written thus lengthens *a*; as,	قرآن	kurān
(3) *Tanwīn* (ً), written above the final vowel shows that *n* is added to it; thus,	فورًا	fauran

The CONSONANTAL SIGNS are:—

(1) *Tashdīd* (ّ), a doubled letter; as,	اِتّفاقًا	ittifākan
(2) *Jazm* (ْ), the letter ends a syllable with no vowel following it; as,	مَرْد	mard
(3) *Wasl* (ٱ), indicates that the consonant is to be joined (in sound) to the previous word, and which only occurs when placed over the Arabic article *al.*	فيِ الْحال	fi-l-hāl

Again, the letters *Alif*, *Dāl*, *Zāl*, *Da*, *Re*, *Ṛa*, *Ze*, *Zhe*, and *Wāo*, it must be noted, do not alter their forms with letters that follow them.

---

* The names of the signs themselves are respectively *zabar* (over), *zer* (below), and *pesh* (before).

PARTS OF SPEECH.

Assuming that the student has made himself thoroughly familiar with the letters of the alphabet, as well as the manner in which vowels combine with consonants, he will now be in a position to study the grammar of the language with advantage. As he proceeds it will agreeably surprise him to find it a less difficult task than he anticipated, for it is an admitted fact that of all the languages in India, Urdū is by far the easiest.

The native Indian grammarians classify the Parts of Speech in their language under *three* heads only, viz., The VERB, the NOUN, and the PARTICLE. But for the purposes of European education it has always been considered an advantage to follow the ordinary classification of the Latin languages as nearly as may be.

We have therefore now to deal with nine Parts of Speech, viz., The Article, Noun, Adjective, Postposition, Pronoun, Verb, Adverb, Conjunction, Interjection.

The Article.

In Hindūstānī, generally speaking, there is no ARTICLE. A simple Noun, as *pādshāh*, signifies either "a king" or "the king." But when greater precision is required there are certain words which serve the purpose, as *ek* (one), *ko'ī* (any one), for the INDEFINITE; *yih* (this), *wuh* (that), with their inflections, for the DEFINITE ARTICLE. Thus:—

ek pādshāh	a king	*ko'ī pādshāh*	any king
yih pādshāh	this king	*wuh pādshāh*	that king.

The Noun.

The Noun has two *Genders* only, and may be considered to have three forms of *Declension*, in each of which the particles *kā*, *ko*, and *se* are used in the following manner:—

Nom.	*beṭā*	a son	*beṭe*	sons
Gen.	*beṭe kā, ke, kī*	of a son	*beṭoṉ kā, ke, kī*	of sons
Dat.	*beṭe ko*	to a son	*beṭoṉ ko*	to sons
Acc.	*beṭā* (or *beṭe ko*)	a son	*beṭe* (or *beṭoṉ ko*)	sons
Voc.	*beṭā* (or *Ai beṭe*)	O son	*beṭo* (or *Ai beṭo*)	O sons
Abl.	*beṭe se*	from a son	*beṭoṉ se*	from sons

From the example given it will be observed the Nominative *beṭā* is changed into *beṭe* in the Singular, and into *beṭoṇ* in the Plural, before the particles *kā*, *ko*, *se*, &c. These slight modifications in the original word are termed the *Oblique* forms.

The use of the particles *kā*, *ke*, *kī*, in the Genitive case, and each signifying "of" in the sense of possession, is regulated by the thing possessed, as in French, thus :—

(a) *Kā*, when it is masculine singular, and in the Nominative case.

(b) *Ke*, when it is masculine singular, and in any case except the Nominative, or when masculine plural in any case.

(c) *Kī*, when it is Feminine, in all cases.

It must also be noted that the Accusative form WITHOUT *ko* is used when the Noun is the *direct* object of the Verb; as :—*Usko ek kitāb do.* Give (to) him a book. The Noun is then said to be in the *Simple Accusative Case.*

But when a special object is particularised the *Accusative* form WITH *ko* is used; as :—*Us kitāb ko paṛho.* Read that book.

Since the particles *kā*, *ke*, *kī*, are uniformly applied to all Nouns, only the Nominative and Oblique forms of the Noun are given in the following table, leaving the Genitive, Dative, Vocative, and Ablative signs to be supplied as they happen to be required.

Properly speaking, the Genitive is an Adjective agreeing with its noun.

First Declension.

All Feminine and Masculine Nouns ending in any letter except *ah*, this *h* being imperceptible.

Nouns of this declension which end in *ā* are Persian or Arabic words, and when Hindī they generally denote relationship, title or profession, &c.

phal, fruit (Masc.).

	Sing.		*Plural.*	
Nom.	*phal*	fruit	*phal*	fruits
Obl.	*phal*	,,	*phaloṇ*	,,

daryā, river, sea (Masc. Persian).

	Sing.		*Plural.*	
Nom.	*daryā*	a river	*daryā*	rivers
Obl.	*daryā*	,,	*daryāoṇ*	,,

dawā, medicine (Fem. Arabic).

	Sing.		*Plural.*	
Nom.	*dawā*	a medicine	*dawāeṇ*	medicines
Obl.	*dawā*	,,	*dawāoṇ*	,,

Hindī words in *ā*, like *chachā*, uncle, and *rājā*, king, are declined like *daryā*.

'aurat, woman (Fem.).

	Sing.		*Plural.*	
Nom.	*'aurat*	a woman	*'aurateṇ*	women
Obl.	*'aurat*	,,	*'auratoṇ*	,,

laṛkī, a girl.

	Sing.		*Plural.*	
Nom.	*laṛkī*	a girl	*laṛkiyāṇ*	girls
Obl.	*laṛkī*	,,	*laṛkiyoṇ*	,,

All Feminine Nouns in *ī* are declined like *laṛkī*.

Second Declension.

All Hindī Masculine Nouns ending in *ā*, except those denoting relationship, title, profession, &c., which belong to the First Declension. All Masculine Nouns ending in *h*.

ghoṛā, horse.

	Sing.		*Plural.*	
Nom.	*ghoṛā*	a horse	*ghoṛe*	horses
Obl.	*ghoṛe*	,,	*ghoṛoṇ*	,,

piyāda, footman.

	Sing.		*Plural.*	
Nom.	*piyāda*	a footman	*piyāde*	footmen
Obl.	*piyāde*	,,	*piyādoṇ*	,,

General Rules for the Inflection of Nouns.

(1) The Oblique Singular and Nominative Plural of all Masculines are alike.

(2) The Oblique Plurals of all Nouns end in *oṇ*, and are

formed by affixing this syllable to the Nominative Singular, or substituting it for the *e* (in those Nouns which have it) of the Nominative Plural, *i.e.*, adding *oṇ* to the inflexible (or radical) part of the word.

(3) Dropping the nasal *ṇ* forms the Vocative Plural.

(4) The Nominative Plural of all Feminines ends in *eṇ*, except those having *ī* in the singular, which for the sake of euphony add *āṇ* (instead of *eṇ*), and thus make the Nominative Plural terminate in *īāṇ*, as:—

beṭī, a daughter; *beṭīāṇ*, daughters:

ī followed by *ā* or *o* is converted into *iy*, thus *beṭīāṇ* = *beṭiyāṇ*.

Rules for Gender.

There are a **Masculine** and a **Feminine**, but no **Neuter**, in the Hindūstānī language, and a few words of **Common** gender. The Gender is regulated partly by nature, partly by termination and grammatical usage, as shown in the foregoing table.

Nouns that are Neuter in English should be taken as Masculine unless they are known to be Feminine.

Words signifying males are Masculine, and females Feminine, whatever may be their terminations.

Feminines.—Most words ending in *ī*, *īṇ*, *sh*, *t*, *ās*, *w*, *r*, *h*, *d*, *k*, *l*, *n*, as also many names of birds and rivers, and monosyllables having medial *ī* or *e*; most pure Sanskrit and Arabic Nouns ending in *ā*; some of the latter in *āh*; likewise Arabic words commencing with *t* and having *ī* in their last syllables, as *tartīb* (order). All Nouns in *ī* (except five) are Feminine, unless Masculine by nature. The exceptions are:—*pānī* (water), *ghī* (clarified butter), *dahī* (curdled milk), *jī* (life), *hāthī* (elephant), *motī* (a pearl), which are Masculine.

Masculines.—All those words not included in the preceding rule as Feminine—subject, however, to many exceptions. But words of the Second Declension, that is, Hindi Nouns ending in *ā*, and Persian Nouns in *a* (*i.e.*, *ah*), also most Nouns ending in *ū* or *o*, are Masculine.

Such words as *ādmī* (a person), *āsāmī* (a client), are naturally of both genders, and some not distinguished by nature, as *fikr* (care), may be used indifferently as belonging to either.

Formation of the Feminine from the Masculine.

Mas.		*Fem.*	
laṛkā	a boy	*laṛkī*	a girl
shāhzāda	a prince	*shāhzādī*	a princess
daswāṇ	tenth (*decimus*)	*daswīṇ*	tenth (*decima*)
malik	a king	*malika*	a queen
nāyak	a lad, a chief	*nāyakā*	a lass
brāhman	a Brahmin	*brāhmanī*	a female of that tribe
dulhā	a bridegroom	*dulhin*	a bride
shā'ir	a poet	*shā'ira*	a poetess
bhā'ī	a brother	*bahin*	a sister
dhobī	a washerman	*dhobin*, *dhoban*	a washerwoman
mullā	a teacher	*mullānī*	an instructress
sher, *sher-nar* (Persian)	a tiger	*shernī*, *sher-māda*	a tigress

Remarks.—(1) Of the numerous methods above exemplified the most important to be recollected is that Masculines in *ā*, when that letter is flexible, as in *laṛkā* (a boy), usually make the Feminine by changing it into *ī*, as:—*laṛkī* (a girl).

(2) Arabic Masculines, as *ṣāḥib* (a gentleman), make the Feminine by adding *ah* (i.e., *a*), as *ṣāḥiba* (a lady.)

(3) Many Nouns in Hindūstānī, as in English, have totally different words for the Masculine and Feminine. Thus:—

bāp	father	*mard*	a man	*bail*	a bull
mā	mother	*'aurat*	a woman	*gā'e*	a cow.

Adjectives.

All Adjectives except those ending in *ā*, and those of Hindī origin, are indeclinable.

Hindī Adjectives ending in *ā* are declined in the Singular and Nominative Plural like Nouns of the Second Declension; but the Oblique Plural is the same as Singular.

The Feminine of these Adjectives (formed by changing *ā* into *ī*) is indeclinable.

Singular.

Nom.	*surkh ghoṛā*(*m.*) a red horse	*surkh ghoṛī*(*f.*) a red mare
Obl.	*surkh ghoṛe*(*m.*) ,,	*surkh ghoṛī*(*f.*) ,,

Plural.

Nom.	*surkh ghoṛe*(*m.*) red horses	*surkh ghoṛiyāṇ*(*f.*) red mares
Obl.	*surkh ghoṛoṇ*(m.) ,,	*surkh ghoṛiyoṇ*(*f.*) ,,

achchhā (*m.*), good. *achchhī* (*f.*), good.

Singular.

Nom.	*achchhā*	good	*achchhī*	good
Obl.	*achchhe*	,,	*achchhī*	,,

Plural.

Nom.	*achchhe*	good	*achchhī*	good
Obl.	*achchhe*	,,	*achchhī*	,,

A few Persian Adjectives ending in *ah* are declined like Hindī Adjectives in *ā*, such as *dīwānah* (mad), *ḥarāmzādah* (low-born, mischievous), *bechārah* (helpless), *kamīnah* (mean). This *h* is omitted in transliteration.

All Adjectives used as Concrete Nouns are declined like Nouns, and, according to their terminations, fall under the two Declensions.

Comparison.

The Hindūstānī Adjective has no variation of form corresponding to the Positive, Comparative, and Superlative in other languages, but the comparison of objects is effected with sufficient precision in the following manner :—

Pos.	*yih ghoṛā achchhā hai.*	This horse is good.
Comp.	*yih ghoṛā us se achchhā hai.*[1]	This horse is better than that.
Super.	*yih ghoṛā sab se achchhā hai.*[2] or *yih ghoṛā sab meṇ achchhā hai*	This horse is best.

If some word equivalent to "compared" be supplied, as understood, these expressions may be literally translated thus :—

Comp. [1]This horse is good (compared) with that.

Super. [2]This horse is good (compared) with all.

Such words as *bahut* (much), *aur*, *ziyāda* (more), &c., are likewise used to heighten the signification of Adjectives, and often merely a re-duplication of the word; thus, *lambā*, long; *aur lambā*, longer; *ziyāda lambā*, too long; *bahut lambā*, *nihāyat lambā*, *lambā*

lambā, very long, &c. Sometimes the Persian terminations for the Comparative and Superlative, *tar* and *tarīn*, are used with words originally Persian, as: *bad*, bad; *badtar*, worse; *badtarīn*, worst; *bih*, good; *bihtar*, better; *bihtarīn*, best.

Postpositions.

What are known as *Prepositions* in English are termed Postpositions in Urdū. They are divided into two classes, Simple and Compound, of which the most important should be immediately committed to memory, as without them hardly a sentence can be formed in the language. Attention to the following explanations will show the manner in which they should be employed:—

(1) In *English* they *always precede* the Noun or Pronoun, while in *Urdū* they *generally follow* them.

(2) The majority follow the Masculine and Feminine Nouns with *ke*, and a few the Feminine Noun with *kī*.

(3) When a word *is itself a Genitive* the particle *ke* or *kī* is omitted, and the Postposition *simple* is added:—

Mere wāsṭe, and not *mere* [*ke*] *wāsṭe* (for my sake).
Tere wāsṭe, and not *tere* [*ke*] *wāsṭe* (for thy sake).
k. wāsṭe, and not *uske* [*ke*] *wāsṭe* (for his sake).

Simple Postpositions.

The most important of these are *kā*, of (for the Masculine); *kī* (for the Feminine); *ko*, to (the sign of the Dative, and also very often of the Accusative); *se* (*seṇ*, *soṇ*, or *satī*), from, with; *meṇ*, in; *par*, on, at; *tak*, *talak*, *lag*, as far as, till.

All these have the common property of governing every Noun and Verb to which they are affixed in the Oblique case. Thus:—

ghoṛī par.	On the mare	(from *ghoṛā*).
larke ko.	To the boy	(,, *laṛkā*).
bolne meṇ	In speaking	(,, *bolnā*).

But *kā*, as the Genitive or Possessive connecting Particle, has the highly important additional property of agreeing, like an adjective-termination, in *gender*, *number*, and *case*, with the governing word or thing possessed. Thus:—

laṛke (or *laṛkī*) *kā ghoṛā.*	The boy's (or girl's) horse.
laṛke (or *laṛkī*) *kī ghoṛī.*	The boy's (or girl's) mare.
laṛkoṇ (or *laṛkīoṇ*) *ke ghoṛe.*	The boys' (or girls') horses.
laṛke (or *laṛkī*) *ke ghoṛe se.*	From the boy's (or girl's) horse.
laṛke (or *laṛkī*) *kī ghoṛī se.*	From the boy's (or girl's) mare.
laṛke (or *laṛkī*) *ke ghoṛoṇ se.*	From the boy's (or girl's) horses.

Compound Postpositions.

Nouns used elliptically (inflected by Simple Postpositions understood, and sometimes expressed) require either a Masculine or Feminine adjunct, according to the *gender* of the Nouns which have been converted to this use. The most generally used are :—

Masculines : *pās, nazdīk, kane,* beside, near ; *sāth,* with, in company of ; *ūpar,* above ; *nīche,* beneath ; *liye, wāsṭe, sabab,* because, or on account of ; *māre,* through ; *sāmne, āge,* before ; *pīchhe, ba'd,* after, behind ; *ware,* on this side; *pare,* on that, beyond; &c.

Feminines : *khāṭir,* for the sake of ; *ṭaraf* (side), towards; *mānind, ṭaraḥ* (manner), like ; *bābat* (subject), about ; *nisbat* (relation), respecting.

Examples :—

ghar ke pās (*meṇ,* in, understood).	Near the house ; *i.e.,* in the vicinity of the house.
laṛke ke sāth (*meṇ*).	With the boy ; *i.e.,* in company of the boy.
uske ta'īn (for *usko*).	To himself ; *i.e.,* his self, or to him.
bāp kī khāṭir.	For the father's sake.
ghar kī ṭaraf.	Towards (to the side of) the house.
mard kī ṭaraḥ.	Like (in the manner of) a man.

In the above and similar examples it is obvious that such words as *meṇ* (in), *ko* (to or for), &c., are understood, and they are even sometimes expressed.

The following is a list of Postpositions most commonly used :—

MASCULINE POSTPOSITIONS WITH "KE."

ke āge,	before.	*ke sāmne,*	before.
ke andar,	within.	*ke sabab,*	because of.
ke ūpar,	above.	*ke siwā,*	except.
ke bā'is,	by reason of.	*ke kane,*	near.
ke barābar,	even with, equal to, by the side of.	*ke gird,*	around.
		ke liye,	for the sake of.
ke ba'd,	after.	*ke pīchhe,*	behind.
ke pār,	over.	*ke wāste,*	on account of.
ke pās,	near.	*ke nīche,*	beneath.
ke ba-ghair,	without.	*ke māre,*	through.
ke tale,	under.	*ke māba'd,*	after.
ke sāth,	with.	*ke nazdīk,*	near.

FEMININE POSTPOSITIONS WITH "KĪ."

kī bābat,	concerning.	*kī tarah,*	like.
kī jihat,	on account of.	*kī ma'rifat,*	through.
kī khātir,	for the sake of.	*kī nisbat,*	relative to.
kī taraf,	towards, on the side of.	*kī zabānī,*	from the report of.

The following Prepositions taken from the Arabic and Persian are of frequent occurrence :—

az,	from.	*bin,* binā,* bilā,*	without.
illā,	except.		
bā,	with, into.	*dar,*	in.
be,	without.	*'alā,*	upon.
bar,	on, in.	*'an,*	from.
fī	in.	*'ind,*	near.
ka,	like.	*li,*	to, for.
ma'a	with.	*min,*	from.

But these particles are chiefly used in connection with words taken from the languages to which they belong.

Pronouns.

These differ materially from the Noun in the mode of their inflection. Pronouns of the first and second person form their Possessive case by *rā*, instead of *kā*; the others take *kā*. They have a distinct objective form, besides the Oblique made with the sign *ko* for the Dative. Thus :—

* These are Urdū words.

Sing.	Nom.	*main*	I
	Gen.	*merā, -re, -rī*	my, of me
	Dat.	*mujhe* (or *mujh ko*)	to me
	Abl.	*mujh se*	from me
Plur.	Nom.	*ham*	We
	Gen.	*hamārā, -re, rī* [(emphatic)	our, of us
	Dat.	*hamen, ham ko, hamen ko*	to us
	Abl.	*ham se, -hamen se* (emphatic)	from us.
Sing.	Nom.	*tū* (or *ta'īn*)	Thou
	Gen.	*terā, re, rī*	thy, of thee
	Dat.	*tujhe* (or *tujh ko*)	to thee
	Abl.	*tujh se*	from thee.
Plur.	Nom.	*tum*	You
	Gen.	*tumhārā, -re, -rī*	your, of you
	Dat.	*tumhen, tum ko*	to you
	Abl.	*tum se*	from you.
Sing.	Nom.	*āp**	Self, *i.e.*, I myself, thou thyself, he himself, &c.
	Poss.	*apnā, -ne, nī*	of self, *i.e.*, of my own, of myself, of thyself, of thy own, &c.
	Dat.	*apne-ko*, &c.	to self, to my, thy, his, her, &c,, self.
Sing.	Nom.	*yih*	This (he, she, it)
	Gen.	*is-kā, -ke, kī*	of this (his, hers, its)
	Dat.	*is-ko, is-e*	to this (him, her, it)
Plur.	Nom.	*ye*	These (or they)
	Gen.	*in-kā, -ke, -kī*	of these (or their)
	Dat.	*in-ko*, or *inhen*	to these (or them).
Sing.	Nom.	*wuh*	That (he, she, it)
	Gen.	*us-kā, -ke, kī*	of that (him, &c.)
	Dat.	*us-ko, us-e*	to that (him, her, it).
Plur.	Nom.	*we*	Those (or they)
	Gen.	*un-kā, ke, kī*	of those (or their)
	Dat.	*un-ko, unhen*	to those (or them).

	Sing.		*Plur.*	
Nom.	*kaun*	Who? which?	*kaun*	Who? which?
Obl.	*kis*	,, ,,	*kinh, kinhon*	,, ,,
Dat.	*kise*	,, ,,	*kinhen*	,, ,,

* *Āp* as an honorific 2nd Personal Pronoun, *i.e.* "your honour," has *āp-kā* for the Genitive, and *āp-ko* for the Dative or Accusative case.

	Sing.		*Plur.*	
Nom.	*jaun, jo*	Who, which	*jaun*	Who, which
Obl.	*jis*	" "	*jin, jinh, jinhoṇ*	" "
Dat.	*jise*	" "	*jinheṇ*	" "
Nom.	*taun, to*	That same	*taun*	Those same.
Obl.	*tis*	" "	*tin, tinh, tinhoṇ*	" "
Dat.	*tise*	" "		
Nom.	*kyā*	What?	(Plural wanting.)	
Obl.	*kāhe*	"		

Nom. *ko'ī* Anyone, any person, or thing. (Applied
Obl. *kisī* chiefly to persons.)

Nom. *kuchh* Anything, something. (Applied chiefly to
Obl. *kisū* things or *mental feelings*, and has generally an *abstract* sense.

Kaun is used of persons as well as things. It may either stand alone or be followed by a Noun.

Jo or *jaun*, the Relative Pronoun, is placed *before* the Noun to which it relates, and forms the first clause; and then the second clause is formed by a Personal Pronoun, as:—

Ask the groom who is on the horse.
Jo *sā'īs ghoṛe par hai*, usse *pūchho*.

Kyā is used of things only. It may either stand alone or be followed by a Noun.

Kuchh or *kisī* is not an interrogative, though the sentence in which either stands may be interrogative.

Interrogation may be expressed :—

(1) By the inflection of the voice.
(2) By the plain interrogative word.
(3) By *kyā* at the beginning of the sentence.

In narration the same Pronouns and Verbs must be used as the original speaker used.

The Verb.*

Verbs in Hindūstānī have only *one conjugation*, and very few irregularities.

Tenses are said to be *Simple* when *no Auxiliary Verb* is

* For list of Verbs see "Hindūstānī Self-Taught," pages 50-55.

employed in forming them, and *Compound* when the *Present* or *Past Participle* of the principal Verb, *together with an Auxiliary*, is used in forming them. It must, however, be noted that what are regarded in English as *Compound—i.e.*, the Future Tense, Present Subjunctive, and the Imperative—are in Hindūstānī *Simple*. Again, it must be borne in mind that, as the Verb *honā*, *i.e.*, "to be," is the *only Auxiliary* in Hindūstānī, it must be generally translated by the Verb *have* in all *Compound Tenses* of the Past Participle.

Every Verb consists of an invariable *stem*, as, for instance, *bolnā*, to speak—*bol* being the stem—and a variable *termination*, as follows :—

Infinitive : —*nā*, to —.

Present Participle : —*tā*, —ing. Past Participle : —*ā*.

Perfect „ —*ke*, *kar*, or *karke* } having —.

TENSES.

	SINGULAR.		PLURAL.	
Subjunc. Pres.	*maiṇ*	—*ūṇ*,	*ham*	—*eṇ*,
	tū	—*e*,	*tum*	—*o*,
	wuh	—*e*,	*we*	—*eṇ*.
Imperative*	*tū*	[stem of verb],	*ham*	—*eṇ*,
			tum	—*o*,
	wuh	—*e*,	*we*	—*eṇ*.
Indic. Future.	*maiṇ*	—*ūṇgā*,†	*ham*	—*eṇge*,
	tū	—*egā*,	*tum*	—*oge*,
	wuh	—*egā*,	*we*	—*eṇge*.
„ Present.	*maiṇ*	—*tā hūṇ*,	*ham*	—*te haiṇ*,
	tū	—*tā hai*,	*tum*	—*te ho*,
	wuh	—*tā hai*,	*we*	—*te haiṇ*.
„ Imperf.	*maiṇ*	—*tā thā*,	*ham*	—*te the*,
	tū	—*tā thā*,	*tum*	—*te the*,
	wuh	—*tā thā*,	*we*	—*te the*.

* In the Imperative Mood there is no First Person Singular :—

		1st Per. Plur.	Let us —
2nd Per. Sing.	— thou	2nd „ „	— ye,
3rd „ „	Let him *or* her —	3rd „ „	Let them —.

† Since a Verb in Hindūstānī agrees with its Nominative in gender as well as in person and number, such parts of the Verb as end in *ā* should be changed into *ī* or *īṇ* as the Nominative is Feminine Singular or Plural

Indic. Past.	1, 2, 3, —*ā*,	1, 2, 3, —*e*.
,, Perfect.	*maiṇ —ā hūṇ*,	*ham —e haiṇ*,
	tū —ā hai,	*tum —e ho*,
	wuh —ā hai,	*we —e haiṇ*.
,, Pluperf.	1,2,3,—*ā thā*,	1, 2, 3, —*ā the*
,, Fu.Per.	*maiṇ —ā hūṇgā*,	*ham —e honge*,
	tū —ā hogā,	*tum —e hoge*,
	wuh —ā hogā,	*we —e honge*.

SPECIAL PARTS.

—*te-hī*, immediately on —ing.
—*iye*, be good enough to —.

As in other tongues generally, the 2nd person Singular of the Imperative is the *root* of the Verb, as :—*bol*, speak (or speak thou). The syllable *nā* added to this forms the Infinitive: *bol-nā*, to speak;

tā, the Present Participle: *bol-tā*, speaking;
ā, the Past: *bol-ā*, spoken.

But when the root ends in a vowel, *y* or *w* is usually inserted, to prevent a hiatus; thus:

pā-nā, to obtain; Past, *pāyā*, instead of *pā-ā*, obtained.

ānā, to come; Future, *āwegā*, instead of *ā-egā*.

Hence, when two *a*'s meet, *y* is inserted, and when *a* and *e* meet, *w* is inserted.

Exceptions.—The following Verbs form the Past irregularly: *jānā* (to go), *gayā* (gone); *karnā* to make or do, *kiyā* (done); *marnā* (to die), *mū'ā* (dead).

From the table already given it will be noticed that from the 2nd person Singular of the Imperative, or root, the remaining persons are formed by adding to it the following affixes: *e, eṇ, o, eṇ.*

The Aorist or Present Subjunctive is nearly the same with the Imperative, being formed by adding the following affixes—*ūṇ, e, e, eṇ, o, eṇ*—to the root.

By again subjoining to the Aorist *gā* for the Singular and *ge* for the Plural the Future Indicative is formed. All the other tenses are made up with the aid of Auxiliaries with the Past and Present Participles. After giving these Auxiliary Tenses (two in number only), which should be studied attentively, and the Auxiliary Verb *honā,* to be, these few rules will be best illustrated by exhibiting the Verb as conjugated in the Active and Passive forms.

Present Tense.

maiṇ hūṇ,	I am,	*ham haiṇ,*	we are,
tū hai,	thou art,	*tum ho,*	you are,
wuh hai	he, she, *or* it is,	*we haiṇ,*	they are.

Past Tense.

maiṇ thā	or	I was,	*ham the*	or	we were,
tū thā	*thī*	thou wast,	*tum the*	*thīṇ*	you were,
wuh thā	(*f.*)	he was,	*we the*	(*f.*)	they were.

Note.—In the Present Tense there is no difference between the Masculine and Feminine genders, but in the Past Tense, when the Nominatives are *Masculine, thā* for singular and *the* for plural are used, and when *Feminine thī* for singular, and for plural *thīṇ.*

The general rule is that in all tenses except the *Aorist* and *Imperative* the Verb must agree with its Nominative in *gender* as well as in *number,* as: *wuh thā,* he was; *wuh thī,* she was.

THE AUXILIARY VERB *honā,* to be *or* become.—Root: *ho.*

Participle Present.	Participle Past.
hotā (fem. *hotī*), being.	*hū'ā* (fem. *hūī*), been.

ROOT TENSES.

Aorist. I be, *or* shall be, *or* should be, &c.

maiṇ ho,ūṇ or *hoṇ*	*ham howeṇ, ho,eṇ,* or *hoṇ*
tū howe, ho,e, or *ho*	*tum ho*
wuh howe, ho,e, or *ho*	*we howeṇ, ho,eṇ,* or *hoṇ.*

Future. I shall *or* will be, &c.

maiṇ ho,ūṇgā, or *hoṇgā* or	*ham howeṇge,* &c.
tū howegā, ho,egā, &c. [*gī*	*tum ho,oge,* &c.
wuh howegā, ho,egā, &c.	*we howeṇge,* &c.

Imperative. Let me be, &c.

maiṇ ho,ūṇ, or *hoṇ*	*ham howeṇ, ho,eṇ* or *hoṇ*
tū howe, ho,e or *ho*	*tum ho*
wuh howe, ho,e or ho	*we howeṇ, ho,eṇ* or *hoṇ.*

Present Participle Tenses.

Indefinite. Had I been, *or* (would that) I had been.

maiṇ / *tū* / *wuh*	*hotā* or *hotī* (f.)	*ham* / *tum* / *we*	*hote* or *hotīṇ* (f.)

Present. I am *or* become.

maiṇ hotā, or *hotī hūn* (f.)	*ham hote*, or *hotī hain* (f.)
tū hotā, or *hotī hai* (f.)	*tum hote*, or *hotī ho* (f.)
wuh hotā, or *hotī hai* (f.)	*we hote*, or *hotī haiṇ* (f.)

Imperfect. I was becoming.

maiṇ / *tū* / *wuh*	*hotā thā* or *hotī thī* (f.)	*ham* / *tum* / *we*	*hote the* or *hotī thīṇ* (f.)

Past Participle Tenses.

Past Indefinite Tense. I was *or* became.

maiṇ / *tū* / *wuh*	*hū,ā*, or *hū,ī* (f.)	*ham*	*hū,e*, or *hū,īṇ* (f.)
		tum / *we*	*hū,e*, or *hū,īṇ* (f.)

Perfect. I have been *or* become.

main hū,ā, or *hū,ī hūn**(f.)	*ham hū,e*, or *hū,ī haiṇ* (f.)
tū hū,ā, or *hū,ī hai* (f.)	*tūm hū,e*, or *hū,ī ho* (f.)
wuh hū,ā, or *hū,ī hai* (f.)	*we hū,e*, or *hū,ī haiṇ* (f.)

Pluperfect. I had been *or* become.

maiṇ / *tū* / *wuh*	*hū,ā thā*, or *hū,ī thī* (f.)	*ham* / *tum* / *we*	*hū,e the*,* or *hū,ī thīṇ* (f.)

The Active Verb.

Infinitive. *Bolnā*, to speak.
Root: *bol*, speak.

Participle Present.	Participle Past.
boltā, speaking.	*bolā*, spoken.

Participle Perfect.

bol, *bol-kar*, *bol-kar ke*, &c., having spoken.

---

* *Note.*—The Compound Tenses of "honā" *are made with* "honā" *as the auxiliary*, the same as any other Verb. Examples:—
Maiṇ hū,ā hūn, I have been. *Ham hū,e the*, We had been.

Imperative.

		bolen,	let us speak,
bol,	speak thou,	*bolo,*	speak (ye),
bole,	let him (her) speak,	*bolen,*	let them speak.

Aorist or Subjunctive.

main bolūn,	I may speak,	*ham bolen,*	we may speak,
tū bole,	thou mayest speak,	*tum bolo,*	you may speak,
wuh bole,	he may speak,	*we bolen,*	they may speak.

Future.

main bolūn-gā,	I shall *or* will speak,	*ham bolenge,*	we shall *or* will speak,
tū bole-gā,	thou shalt *or* wilt speak.	*tum bolo-ge,*	you will speak,
wuh bole-gā,	he shall *or* will speak,	*we bolen-ge,*	they will speak.

Present.

*main boltā hūn**,	I am speaking.	*ham bolte hain,*	we are speaking.
tū boltā hai,	thou art speaking.	*tum bolte ho,*	you are speaking.
wuh boltā hai,	he is speaking.	*we bolte hain,*	they are speaking.

Imperfect.

main boltā thā,	I was speaking.	*ham bolte the,*	we were speaking.
tū boltā thā,	thou wast speaking.	*tum bolte the,*	you were speaking.
wuh boltā thā,	he was speaking.	*we bolte the,*	they were speaking.

Perfect.

main bolā hūn,	I have spoken.	*ham bole hain,*	we have spoken.
tū bolā hai,	thou hast spoken.	*tum bole ho,*	you have spoken.
wuh bolā hai,	he has spoken.	*we bole hain,*	they have spoken.

Past Indefinite.

main bolā,	I spoke,	*ham bole,*	we spoke,
tū bolā,	thou spokest,	*tum bole,*	you spoke,
wuh bolā,	he spoke,	*we bole,*	they spoke.

* ***Note.*—The Auxiliary Verb is placed last in Hindōstānī.**

Pluperfect.

maiṇ bolā thā, I had		*ham bole the,*	we had	
tū bolā thā, thou hadst	spoken.	*tum bole the,*	you had	spoken.
wuh bolā thā, he had		*we bole the,*	they had	

Conditional.

maiṇ boltā,	*ham bolte,*
tū boltā,	*tum bolte,*
wuh boltā,	*we bolte,*

may be translated, according to the context, either "Had I spoken," or "I might (or would) have spoken." This form is also an Indefinite Present; thus, *maiṇ boltā* means generally, "I speak," by the omission of *hūṇ*.

The compound tenses are formed by the addition of the Auxiliary Verb to the Present or Past Participle, as:—*maiṇ hūṇ*, I am; *maiṇ boltā hūṇ*, I am speaking; *maiṇ bolā hūṇ*, I have spoken. This shows that when the Auxiliary Verb is added to the *Present* Participle it is translated by the Verb *to be*, but when added to the *Past* Participle it is translated by the Verb *to have*.

The Particle "Ne."

One of the difficulties of the Hindūstānī language is the use of the particle *ne* (by). In the tenses of an Active Transitive Verb in which the Past Participle occurs, as *mārā*, the Agents of the Verb require to be indicated by this particle *ne* affixed to and usually inflecting them* as a Postposition, while the Verb itself (*i.e.*, the Participle and Auxiliary) agrees in *gender* and *number* with its object; unless the latter be distinguished by the sign *ko*, in which case the Verb remains *impersonal* in the Masculine Singular, thus:—

Perfect Tense.

maiṇ	*ne*	I have struck,	*ham*	*ne*	we have struck,
tū	*mārā*	thou hast ,,	*tum*	*mārā*	you have ,,
us†	*hai,*	he has ,,	*unhoṇ*	*hai,*	they have ,,

* Except *maiṇ* and *taiṇ* or *tū*, which are not inflected by *ne*, but retain their Nominative form; and they thus correspond with their Plurals *ham* and *tum*, which, though they admit of inflection, usually dispense with it.

† *Us* and *unhoṇ* are the inflected forms of *wuh* and *we* used as above.

Past Indefinite.

maiṇ	*ne*	I struck,	*ham*	*ne*	we struck,
tū	*mārā,*	thou struckest,	*tum*	*mārā,*	you struck,
us		he struck,	*unhoṇ*		they struck.

Pluperfect.

maiṇ	*ne*	I had struck,	*ham*	*ne*	we had struck,
tū	*mārā*	thou hadst ,,	*tum*	*mārā*	you had ,,
us	*thā,*	he had ,,	*unhoṇ*	*thā,*	they had ,,

Note.—According to the gender and number of the object of the Verb (here not stated) the Participle *mārā* becomes *māre* (Mas. Plu.), *mārī* (Fem. Sing.), *mārīṇ* (Fem. Plu.); and *thā* in like manner becomes *the*, *thī*, *thīṇ*, as in the following examples:—

laṛke ne chiṛiyā mārī,	The boy killed the bird.
laṛkīoṇ ne chiṛiyā mārī,	The girls killed the bird.
laṛkoṇ ne chiṛiyān mārīṇ; or *laṛkoṇ ne chiṛiyoṇ ko mārā*	The boys killed the birds.

The particle *ne* must not be mistaken for a negative (*nahīn*, not), as in reality it is an affirmative. This construction is a source of much perplexity to the beginner, and must be carefully studied by those who want thoroughly to master the language. The particle *ne* is properly defined to be the indispensable symbol of the agent of the active Preterite.

The Passive Voice.

The tenses of the Passive Voice are regularly formed in all Transitive Verbs by means of the tenses of the Verb *jānā*, to go, with the Past Participle.

Passive Verb Inf.	*mārā jānā,*	to be killed.
Part. Present.	*mārā jātā,*	being killed.
Part. Passive.	*mārā gayā,*	been killed.

Imperative.

Sing.		*Plural.*	
tū mārā jā,	be thou killed.	*tum māre jā'o,*	be you killed.

Aorist or Subjunctive.

Sing.	*Plural.*
maiṇ mārā jāūṇ,	*ham māre jāweṇ,* or *jā'eṇ,*
tū mārā jāwe, or *jā'e*	*tum mārā jā'o,*
wuh mārā jāwe, or *jā'e,*	*we māre jāweṇ,* or *jā'eṇ.*

Other tenses are formed similarly. If the nominative of the Verb be Feminine, the terminations of the Passive Participle, and of the participial forms of the Future of the Auxiliary must be changed to *ī*, both in the singular and plural.

When the Imperative mood is used to a superior, the respectful form is employed, which is made by adding *iye* (be pleased) to the root; thus,

boliye (from *bolnā*),	be pleased to speak;
kījiye (from *karnā*),	be pleased to do;
lījiye (from *lenā*),	please take;
dījiye (from *denā*),	please give.

THE VERB *jānā*, To Go.

In all its tenses *jānā*, to go, is conjugated like *bolnā*, before exemplified, except that its Past is formed irregularly, and that the root *jā* ending in a vowel requires *w* in the Imperative or Aorist, and sometimes in the Future, to prevent a hiatus. The Past Participle of the Verb conjugated is uniformly inserted thus after the Pronoun or Nominative, and agrees with it in gender and number—a rule of concord which applies also to *thā* (was) and all other Participles.

Compound Tenses of the Present Participle.

Present.	*maiṇ jātā hūṇ,*	I am going.
	ham jāte haiṇ,	we are going.
Imperfect.	*maiṇ jātā thā,*	I was going.
	ham jāte the,	we were going.
Future.	*maiṇ jātā hoūngā,*	I shall be going.
	ham jāte howenge,	we shall be going.

Compound Tenses of the Past Participle.

Present.	*maiṇ gayā hūṇ,*	I have gone.
	ham gaye haiṇ,	we have gone.
Imperfect.	*maiṇ gayā thā,*	I was gone.
	ham gaye the,	we were gone.
Future.	*maiṇ gayā hoūngā,*	I shall have gone.
	ham gaye hoenge,	we shall have gone.

An important Verb of frequent occurrence in Hindūstānī is the Active Verb—

Karnā, To Do, or Make. Root: *kar*.

Infinitive: *karnā*, to do; *karne kā, ke, kī*, of doing.

Participle Present.	Participle Past.
kartā, doing.	*kiyā*, done.

Participle Perfect: *karke, karkar*,* having done.

Imperative: *kar*, do thou.

Aorist or Subjunctive.

maiṇ karūṇ,	I may do,	*ham kareṇ*,	we may do,
tū kare,	thou mayest do,	*tum karo*,	you may do,
wuh kare,	he may do,	*we kareṇ*,	they may do.

Future.

maiṇ karūṇgā,	I shall do,	*ham kareṇge*,	we shall do,
tū karegā,	thou shalt do,	*tum karoge*,	you shall do,
wuh karegā,	he shall do,	*we kareṇge*,	they shall do.

Conditional.

maiṇ kartā,	I would do,	*ham karte*,	we would do.
tū kartā,	thou wouldst do,	*tum karte*,	you would do.
wuh kartā,	he would do,	*we karte*,	they would do.

Derivative Verbs.

(1) Causals may be regularly formed from every Verb in the language. If the root is intransitive the Causal will be the transitive form of the Verb, but if the root is transitive the Causal will be doubly transitive or causative. Generally the Causal is formed by the addition of *ā* to the root, and the double Causal by adding *wā*; thus,

Verb: *pak-nā*,	to grow ripe, to be cooking.
Active: *pak-ānā*,	to make ripe, or, to cook.
Causal: *pak-wānā*,	to cause others to cook.

N.B.—When the medial vowel of the root is long it becomes short in the Active and Causal; thus,

bolnā,	to speak.	*bulānā*,	to call.
sīkhnā,	to learn.	*sikhānā*	to teach.

* The participle in *kar* or *ke*, &c. (sometimes *karkar* or *karke*, all being derived from *karnā*, sometimes only the plain stem *kar*), is used to avoid the repetition of *aur* (and), as

Yih bāt bolkar (or karkar or karke) *chalā gayā*,
Having said this, he went away, *or*, He said this much and left.

(2) In other cases the medial vowel is merely lengthened to form the Active; thus,

palnā,	to thrive.	*pālnā,*	to nourish.
khulnā,	to expand.	*kholnā,*	to open.

(3) By adding *lānā* (instead of *ānā*) to the root, particularly when the latter ends in a long vowel; thus,

khānā,	to eat.	*khilānā,*	to feed.
sonā,	to sleep.	*sulānā,*	to lull asleep.

In the double Causal *lā* becomes *lwā*: *khilwānā,* to cause to feed; *sulwānā,* to cause to sleep. And many are formed both ways, as from *sīkhnā,* to learn, *sikhānā* and *sikhlānā,* to teach. Some take only the form of the double Causal as *gānā,* to sing; *gawānā,* cause to sing. Some are formed irregularly; as,

biknā,	to be sold.	*bechnā,*	to sell.
rahnā,	to stay.	*rakhnā,*	to place.
ṭūṭnā,	to be broken.	*toṛnā,*	to break.

Compound Verbs.

Generally speaking, Compound Verbs are formed by adding a second Verb regularly conjugated, either

(1) The Root,
(2) ,, Past Participle,
(3) ,, Inflected Infinitive.

of another Verb. In some cases, the second Verb drops its *primary signification;* thus,

mārnā, to strike + *ḍālnā,* to throw = *mār-ḍālnā,* to kill.
marnā, ,, die + *jānā,* ,, go = *mar-jānā,* ,, die.
khānā, ,, eat + *jānā,* ,, go = *khā-jānā,* ,, eat up.

In such cases the second Verb is said to *intensify* or *strengthen* the meaning of the *Root,* &c., prefixed, and it *only* is conjugated.

The following are the most commonly used to form Compound Verbs:—

uṭhnā	to rise.	*pānā,*	to be allowed.
jānā,	,, go.	*lagnā,*	,, begin.
denā,	,, give.	*saknā,*	,, be able.
lenā,	,, take.	*chuknā,*	,, finish.
ḍālnā,	,, throw.	*paṛnā,*	,, fall.

Potentials.

Potentials are Compound Verbs which express ability to do a thing. They are formed by adding the Verb *saknā* (to be able) to the root; thus,

karnā,	to do.	*kar saknā,*	to be able to do.
bolnā,	to speak.	*bol saknā,*	to be able to speak.

Completives.

These Compound Verbs are formed by adding the Verb *chuknā* (to be finished) to the root; thus,

bolnā,	to speak.	*bol chuknā,*	to have finished speaking.
karnā,	to do.	*kar chuknā,*	to have finished doing.

Intensives.

Intensives are formed by prefixing the root of a verb to certain other verbs determined by usage, these latter being conjugated regularly, whilst the root remains unchanged; thus,

pīnā,	to drink.	*pī jānā,*	to drink up.
kāṭnā,	to cut.	*kāṭ ḍālnā,*	to cut up.
girnā,	to fall.	*gir paṛnā,*	to tumble down.

Notes on Verbs.

(1) An Active Verb takes sometimes a Dative and sometimes a Nominative form of the object. The former is generally used in speaking of persons; the latter of things. But if an inanimate object is particularised the Dative form is used, which may be seen by referring to p. 15.

(2) A certain number of verbal expressions, which can scarcely be called Compound Verbs, are formed by adding certain Verbs to the present and past participles of Verbs. Thus, Verbs *jānā,* to go, *rahnā,* to remain, and *honā,* to be, added to the Present Participles form phrases which have a continuative and habitual sense. The Participle is placed in the Oblique Case, and is used adverbially; thus,

likhnā,	to write.	*likhte jānā,*	to go on writing.
gānā,	to sing	*gāte rahnā,*	to continue singing.

(3) Similarly phrases with a habitual sense are made by adding *karnā* (to do) to the Past Participle; thus,

bolnā, to speak.	*bolā karnā*, to be in the habit of speaking.
ronā, to cry.	*royā karnā*, to be in the habit of crying.

(4) The inflected Infinitive with certain Verbs makes a number of useful compounds. These are:—

(*a*) Inceptives formed by adding the Verb *lagnā*, to come in contact, to touch. Thus, *bolnā*, to speak; *bolne lagnā*, to commence speaking.

(*b*) Permissives formed by adding the Verb *denā*, to give: *bolnā*, to speak; *bolne denā*, to allow to speak.

(*c*) Acquisitives, in the sense of obtaining leave to do something, by adding the Verb *pānā*, to find; *ānā*, to come; *āne pānā*, to get leave to come.

(5) Desideratives are formed by adding the Verb *chāhnā*, to desire, to wish, to the Infinitive *jānā*, to go; *jānā chāhnā*, to wish to go.

(6) Verbal Nouns of agency are formed by changing *nā* of the Infinitive Verb into *ne*, and affixing *wālā* for the Masculine and *wālī* for the Feminine; as *likhne-wālā*, male writer; *likhne-wālī*, female writer.

(7) The English idioms, "It is," "There is," "There are," are expressed in Hindūstānī by the Substantive Verb *hai* and (pl.) *haiṇ*.

(8) In expressing the time of day the Verb *bajnā*, to sound, should always be used; as,

What o'clock is it?	*kyā bajā hai!*
Two.	*do baje.*
A quarter past two.	*sawā do baje.*
Half-past two.	*aṛhāī-baje*
A quarter to three.	*paune tīn baje.*
Half-past three.	*sāṛhe tīn baje.*

Adverbs.*

In Hindūstānī, as in English, Adverbs are sometimes formed by using Adjectives. They are also made by adding the Postposition *se* to certain Nouns; as, *zor* (strength), *zor se* (forcibly).

---

* For list of Adverbs see "Hindūstani Self-Taught," pages 56-60.

Adverbs *generally* should precede the Verb or Adjective they modify, yet in certain cases their proper place is at the end of a sentence; this remark applying particularly to the Negative Adverb *nahīṇ* (= *na hai*, not is).

The following POSTPOSITIONS are employed as Adverbs:—

āge,	in front.	*darmiyān,*	in the midst.	*nīche,*	under.
andar,	inside.	*gird,*	around.	*pīchhe,*	behind.
bāhar,	outside.	*ḳarīb,*	near.	*sāmne,*	in front [of.
bīch,	among.	*nazdīk,*	,,	*ūpar,*	above.

The most useful Adverbs are formed from the five Pronouns, *yih* (this), *wuh* (that), *kaun?* (the Interrogative "who?" "which?"), *jaun* (the Relative "who," "which"), and *taun* (the Correlative) with certain significant suffixes. Thus:—

PRONOUN	*yih* This	*wuh* That	*kaun?* Who? which?	*jaun* What, which	*taun* That

which form the Adverbs of—

Quality	*aisā* Such, like this	*waisā* Like that	*kaisā?* Like what? how?	*jaisā* Like which	*taisā* Like the same
Quantity	*itnā* This much	*utnā* That much	*kitnā* How much?	*jitnā* As much	*titnā* So much
Number	*itne* This many	*utne* That many	*kitne?* How many?	*jitne* As many	*titne* So many
Mode	*yūṇ* Thus	*wūṇ* In that manner	*kyūṇ?* How?	*jyūṇ* As	*tyūṇ* So
Place	*yahāṇ,* *idhar* Here, hither	*wahāṇ* *udhar* There, thither	*kahāṇ?* *kidhar?* Where? whither?	*jahāṇ,* *jidhar* Where, whither	*tahāṇ,* *tidhar* In that same place
Time	*ab* Now	(*us-waḳt*) (Then)	*kab?** When?	*jab** When	*tab** Then

* The vulgar forms *kad, jad, tad* respectively, are not much in use.

Compound Adverbs.

ab-tak, *ab-talak*,	till now, still.	*idhar udhar*, *jidhar tidhar*,	here and there.
jab-tak,	as long as.	*jahāṇ jahāṇ*,	wherever.
kab-tak?	how long?	*jab kabhī*	whenever.
kabhī-kabhī,	sometimes.		

Adverbs of Time.

kal,	to-morrow *or* yesterday.
parsoṇ,	the day after to-morrow, *or* the day before yesterday.
tarsoṇ,	the third day to come.
narsoṇ,	the fourth day from this.

Adverbs from the Persian.

ḳazārā,	by chance.	*shāyad*,	perhaps.
chigūna,	how.	*k͟hwāh na k͟hwāh*,	positively.
ek-bār,	once.		
bārhā (pl.)	often.		

Adverbs from the Arabic.

albatta,	certainly.	*fi-l-ḥāl*,	at present.
al-g͟haraẓ,	in short.	*fi-l-faur*,	instantly.
alḥāl,	at this time.	*ittifāḳan*,	by chance.
aṣlan, ***aṣlā***,	by no means.	*k͟huṣūṣan*,	especially.
		maṣalan,	for example.
wa g͟haira,	and so forth, etc.	*faḳaṭ*,	merely, only.

Conjunctions.*

In Hindūstānī, Conjunctions are employed exactly as in English. The following list embraces those most commonly used :—

aur, *o*,	and.	*bajuz*,	except.
jo, agar,	if.	*lekin*, *magar*,	but.
war,	and if.	*balki*	moreover, nay, besides.
agarchi	although.		
illā,	if not.	*par*,	but, yet.

* For list of Conjunctions see "Hindūstānī Self-Taught," pages 56-60.

bhī,	also, even.	*goyā,*	as if.
to, pas,	then, therefore.	*nahīṇ to,*	if not, otherwise.
ki,	that, thus, as, whether, or.	*harchand,*	although, however much.
kyūnki,	because.	*khwāh,*	whether.
go-ki,	although.	*yā,*	either, or.

Interjections.

The Interjection follows the English usage, and it is unnecessary therefore to do more than give a list of those ordinarily employed.

shābāsh,	Bravo! well done!
āfrīn,	Praise on you! bravo!
wāh-wāh,	Admirable! well done!
kyā-khūb,	How excellent!
dhan-i-dhan,	How fortunate!
wāh jī! / *kyā-bāt hai!*	What, sir! what a thing! how admirable! (Expressions of admiration.)
bāp re,	Astonishing! dreadful!
hā,e hā,e, / *wā,e wā,e,*	Alas! woe to me!
hat, chhī-chhī,	Hush! fie!
ai, o,	Oh!
re, are,†	Holla!
hāṇ, or hūṇ,	Yes.
achchhā, khair,	Very good! well!
jī, jī-hāṇ,	Yes (in a respectful manner).
wā-wailā!	Woe! alas!
ḥaif, afsos!	Alas!
āhā! oho!	Oh! strange!

† *Ari,* if a female is addressed.

Prefixes & Suffixes.

By means of "PREFIXES" and "SUFFIXES" to Nouns and Adjectives, a large number of other words are formed; *e.g.*,

Bū (smell), bad*bū* (a bad smell).
Angrez (an Englishman), *angrezī* (English).
Dūkān (a shop); *dūkān*dār (a shopkeeper), *dūkāndārī* (shopkeeping).

The following is a list of PREFIXES in common use:—

Ba. At, with, by; *e.g.*,
basar, at or to a head or end;
baṭaur, by way of.

Bad. Bad.
badḳismat, bad luck;
badnām, bad repute;
badshakl, ill-formed;
badnaṣībī, misfortune.

Be. Without.
befikr, without care;
behosh, senseless;
behūdah, absurd;
bejān, lifeless;
beshakk, beyond a doubt;
besharm, shameless;
beḳuṣūr, without blame;
bewuḳūf, without experience (stupid).

Bi [Arabic]. In, on.
bi'l fi'l, for the present;
bi'l kull, on the whole, entirely;
bi'l 'aks, on the contrary.

Fī [Arabic]. Each, "per," in.
fi'l-jumla, in the total;
fi'l-ḥāl, in the present;
fi'l-ḥaḳīḳat, in truth;
fi'l-wāḳi', in reality;
fi'l-faur, instantly.

Ghair, wanting, deficient.
ghair-ḥāẓir, absent;
ghair-mumkin, impossible.

Har. Each, every.
har-ek, each one;
har-roz, every day (daily).

Kam. Deficient.
kam-'aḳl, of deficient sense;
kam-bakht, unfortunate;
kam-'aḳlī, devoid of sense.

Khush. Pleased, satisfied.
khush-āwāz, sweet-voiced;
khush-bū, sweet smell;
khush-ḥāl, in happy circumstances;
khush-zabān, honey-tongued;
khush-dil, pleased at heart.

Lā. Destitute of.
lā-jawāb, without an answer;
lā-chār, helpless;
lā-khirāj, rent-free;
lā-parwā, without care;
lā-wāriṣ, heirless.

Mahā. Great.
mahā-rājā, great king;
mahā-rānī, great queen;
mahā-nadī, great river;
mahā-jan (the great person), banker, merchant.

Nā. No, not.
nā-dānī, want of wisdom;
nā-durust, not right;
nā-ma'lūm, unknown;
nā-pasand, not approved;
nā-rāst, unjust, unrighteous;
nā-wāḳif, uninformed.

The SUFFIXES in the language are not nearly so plentiful as the PREFIXES. The following list comprises those that are most commonly used :—

Dān. A vessel for holding anything.
gul-dān, a flower-vase ;
ṣābundān, a soap dish ;
chā'e-dān, a tea-caddy ;
pāo-dān, a footstool.

Dār, *Gār*, or *Gar*. Agent.
chaukīdār, a watchman ;
khidmatgār, a servant ;
sar-dār (head-man), chief ;
ḳarẓ-dār, debtor ;
saudā-gar, trader ;
ṣūbah-dār, governor ;
taḥṣīl-dār, collector of rents ;
thāna-dar, an officer in charge of police-station ;
ṭhīke-dār, leaseholder ; contractor ;
zamīn-dār, landholder.

Gāh. Place.
shikār-gāh, hunting ground ;
bār-gāh, place of audience, darbar ;
razm-gāh, place of battle ;
gend-gāh, racquet-court.

I. State, quality, position, &c.
bhalā'ī, goodness ;
bhār-ī, heavy ;
ṣafā'ī, cleanliness ;
saudāgar-ī, trade ;
shikār-ī, hunter ;
taḥṣīldār-ī, the area of a rent collector ;
zamīndārī, landed property.

Jāma. Cloth.
mom-jāma, wax-cloth.

Khāna. A place where work is done or things are kept, or room.
lohār-khāna, blacksmith's shop ;
bāwarchi-khāna, cookhouse (kitchen) ;
ghusl-khāna, bath-room.

Mand. Full of.
fā'ida-mand, advantageous ;
daulat-mand, wealthy ;
fikr-mand, thoughtful.

Nāma. A writing.
hiba-nāma, a deed of gift ;
ṣulḥ-nāma, a deed settling a dispute.

Sā. Like, rather.
bandar-sā, monkey-like ;
mard-sā, manly ;
'aurat-sā, effeminate ;
baṛā-sā, rather large ;
chhoṭā-sā, rather small.

Se. Manner.
zor-se, forcibly ;
khabardārī-se, carefully.

Wālā or *Wālī*. Person.
pankhā-wālā, a pankha-puller ;
roṭī-wālā, baker ;
machhlī-wālā, fishmonger ;
nāch-wālī, female dancer ;
dūdh-wālī, milk-woman.

Note.—The suffixes such as "ābād," "nagar," and "pūr" are used solely as terminations of Indian towns and cities ; *e.g.*,

"Allāh-ābād."	The city of		Allah, or God.
"Aurung-ābād."	,,	,,	Aurungzebe.
"Ahmadnagar."	,,	,,	Ahmad.
"Nāg-pūr."	,,	,,	Nāg, or snakes ; &c.

Numerals.

The Hindūstānī numerals are derived from the Sanskrit. They precede the Noun, which may be put either in the singular or the plural number.

When the Noun denotes time, distance, direction, measure or quality it is generally put in the singular; thus,

chār gaz kapṛā, four yards of cloth.
sāṭh baras, sixty years.

In all other cases the plural is more commonly used:

chār kitābeṇ, four books.

The numbers above one hundred are formed as in English, but without the Conjunction; thus,

ek sau chār, one hundred and four.

Cardinals.

1	*ek*
2	*do*
3	*tīn*
4	*chār*
5	*pānch*
6	*chha*
7	*sāt*
8	*āṭh*
9	*nau*
10	*das*
11	*igārah, gyārah*
12	*bārah*
13	*terah*
14	*chaudah*
15	*pandrah*
16	*solah*
17	*satrah*
18	*aṭhārah*
19	*unīs, unnīs*
20	*bīs*
21	*ikkīs*
22	*bā'īs*
23	*te'īs*
24	*chaubīs*
25	*pachīs*
26	*chhabbīs*
27	*satā'īs*
28	*aṭhāīs*
29	*untīs*
30	*tīs*
31	*iktīs*
32	*battīs*
33	*tetīs, taiṇtīs*
34	*chautīs*
35	*paiṇtīs*
36	*chhattīs*
37	*saiṇtīs*
38	*aṭhtīs, aṛtīs*
39	*untālīs unchālīs*
40	*chālīs*
41	*ektālīs, iktālīs*
42	*be'ālīs*
43	*te'tālīs*
44	*chau'ālīs*
45	*paintālīs*
46	*chhi'ālīs*
47	*saiṇtālīs*
48	*aṛtālīs, aṭhtālīs*
49	*unchās*
50	*pachās*
51	*ekāwan, ikāwan*
52	*bāwan*
53	*tirpan*
54	*chauwan*
55	*pachpan*
56	*chhapan*
57	*sattāwan*
58	*aṭhāwan*
59	*unsaṭh*
60	*sāṭh*
61	*eksāṭh, iksaṭh*
62	*bāsaṭh*
63	*tirsaṭh*
64	*chausaṭh*
65	*paiṇsaṭh*
66	*chhiyāsaṭh*
67	*saṛsaṭh*
68	*aṭhsaṭh, aṛsaṭh*
69	*unhattar*
70	*sattar*
71	*ekhattar*
72	*bahattar*
73	*tihattar*
74	*chauhattar*
75	*pachhattar*
76	*chhihattar*
77	*sathattar*
78	*aṭhhattar*

79 *unāsī*	92 *bānawe, biyā-nawe*	100 *sau*
80 *assī*	93 *tirānawe, tira-nawwe*	101 *ek sau ek*
81 *ekāsī*	94 *chaurānawe*	110 *ek sau das*
82 *be'āsī*	95 *pachānawe, paṇchānawe*	200 *do sau*
83 *tirāsī*	96 *chhiyānawe, chhānawe*	300 *tīn sau*
84 *chaurāsī*	97 *satānawe*	400 *chār sau*
85 *pachāsī*	98 *aṭhānawe*	500 *pānch sau*
86 *chhiāsī*	99 *ninānawe, navā-nawe*	a thousand, *hazār*, *das sau*
87 *satāsī*		a million, *das lākh*
88 *aṭhāsī*		ten million, *kṛoṛ*
89 *nawāsī*		
90 *nawwe*		
91 *ekānawe*		

ORDINALS.

The first four Ordinals are irregularly made, but from the fifth upwards they are regularly formed by adding *wāṇ* to the Cardinal number, and are inflected like Adjectives.

sāt, seven; *sātwāṇ* (m.), *sātwīṇ* (f.), *sātweṇ* (oblique), seventh.

1st	*pahlā*	6th	*chhaṭhā*	11th	*igārahwāṇ* *gyārahwāṇ*
2nd	*dūsrā*	7th	*sātwāṇ*	12th	*bārahwāṇ*
3rd	*tīsrā*	8th	*āṭhwāṇ*	21st	*ekīswāṇ*
4th	*chauthā*	9th	*nawāṇ*	100th	*sawāṇ*
5th	*pānchwāṇ*	10th	*daswāṇ*	last	*pichhlā*

In Compound Numbers the termination *wāṇ* is added to the last number of the compound only, as:—

ek-sau-bīswāṇ, one hundred and twentieth.

DISTRIBUTIVE NUMERALS are formed by repeating the Cardinal number: thus, *ek ek*, one at a time, one apiece; *chār chār*, four at a time, four apiece.

MULTIPLICATIVES are formed by adding the word *gunā*, (f. *gunī*) to the Cardinals; thus, *dogunā*, twice, shortened into *dūnā*; *chārgunā* or *chaugunā*, fourfold, four times.

Also by adding *harā* (f. *harī*); *doharā* or *duhrā*, twofold.

Part II.

EXERCISES AND EXAMINATION PAPERS.

INCLUDING A HINDŪSTĀNĪ TRANSLATION OF

THE LORD'S PRAYER

AND

A POEM BY MR. RUDYARD KIPLING.

The *literal* interlinear English translation is provided throughout these Exercises, it being unnecessary to encumber the work with the English grammatical renderings also; but special foot-notes are given in many cases to further explain the Hindūstānī, where the form of composition is particularly involved to an European student.

A few remarks regarding the idioms of the language will not be out of place here, and will assist the student in going through the following phrases, exercises, &c. He may thus be able to take special note of them as they occur.

(1) The period of the duration of time, or the amount of space, time, weight or measure is put in the Nominative case; the point of time of the occurrence of an event, or the price at which anything is bought or sold, in the Dative case; whilst the limit of time, space, price or measure is indicated by the postposition *tak* "up to."

(2) In such phrases as "a plate *of* meat," &c., *of* is omitted.

(3) Such phrases as "*fell from*," "*out of*," are rendered "fell from *on*" and "*from in*" (inside).

(4) The *Pluperfect Tense* is used for our plain *Past*.

(5) The *Aorist Tense* for the *Subjunctive Mood*.

(6) In phrases where *till* or *since* are used they must be always rendered by a Negative before the Verb of the first clause. The reason of this is, that *we* fix our minds on the moment of our *return*, *the natives* on the duration of the *absence*.

(7) The word *ghanṭā* (a bell) is used to mean "an hour."

(8) In using numerals *and* is left untranslated.

(9) Omission of Pronouns where no ambiguity is caused.

(10) Doubling words in order to strengthen the force.

(11) Genitives and Datives come, in order, before the Accusative.

(12) Compound Verbs should be used in preference to Simple Verbs.

(13) Passive Voice should never be used when the Active Voice can express the meaning.

(14) Distribution is marked by doubling the numeral.

(15) To express *purpose*, *intention*, or *object* the inflected form of the Infinitive is followed by *ko* or *ke wāste*.

(15) When speaking of persons of distinction the *Verb* is put in the *plural*, even though the *Nominative* be *singular*.

EXERCISES. (*Sabaḳ.*)

Specially Adapted for Private Study.

[The words used in these Exercises are mostly taken from the Vocabularies in "Hindūstānī Self-Taught" as indicated.]

1.

(Vocabularies 1—3, pages 15—17.*)

Khudā ne āsmān aur prithwī ko[1] *paidā kiyā.*[2] *Sūraj pūrab*
By God Heaven and Earth created made. Sun East

meṇ uṭhtā aur pachcham meṇ ḍūb jātā hai.[3] *Thoṛe dinoṇ meṇ*
in rises and West in sink goes. Few days in

chāṇd-grahan hogā.[4] *Zamīn par shabnam hai. Hawā*
moon-eclipse will be. The ground on dew is. Wind

bahut chaltī hai,[5] *ṭūfān ho'egā.*[6] *Dhanak ko dekho kaisī*
much blowing is, storm will be. The rainbow at look thou how

k͟hūb-ṣūrat hai.[7] *Is nadī kā dhārā bahut zorāwar hai.*
beautiful is. This river of the current very strong is.

Har roz samundar meṇ jawār aur bhāṭhā hotā hai. Hindūstān
Every day the sea flows and ebbs. India

ke kināre ke nazdīk bahut pahāṛ haiṇ. Sonā chāndī se
of the shores near many rocks are. Gold, silver

aur tāmbe se[8] *ziyāda ḳīmatī hai. Almās, motiyoṇ se,*
and copper from, more valuable is. Diamonds, pearls

lāl se aur zumurrud se besh-ḳīmatī haiṇ. Pītal, lohā, sīsā
rubies or emeralds from, more precious are. Brass, iron, lead,

aur ḳalaī kām ke dhāt haiṇ.
and tin (use of)[9] metals are.

[1]Postposition showing the Objective case. [2]Were created. [3]Sets. [4]*There* understood. [5]Very high. [6]There will be, or, We shall have. [7]*It* understood. [8]Gold compared with. [9]Useful.

2.

(Vocabularies 4—6, pages 18—22.*)

Hindūstān meṇ jānwar aur chiṛiyāṇ bahuterī haiṇ.[1] *Ghoṛe*
India in animals and birds very many are. Horses

aur kutte hoshyār jānwar haiṇ. Gā'e, bheṛī aur hāthī
and dogs sagacious animals are. Cows, sheep and elephants

ādmī ke liye mufīd haiṇ. Toṭe, tadarv aur kabūtar ke
to mankind use of are. Parrots, pheasants and pigeons of

* See "Hindūstānī Self-Taught."

par khūb-ṣūrat hain. Hindūstān men bāgh aur singh bil-fi'l
feathers beautiful are. India in tigers and lions now

kamyāb hain. Shahd kī makkhiyān mihnatī kīre hain. Sāmp
scarce are. Honey-bees industrious insects are. Snakes

zahrīle hasharāt hain. Nāg kā dānt aksar kātil hai. Seb,
venomous reptiles are. A viper of the sting often fatal is. Apples,

anjīr aur angūr achchhe phal hain. Gulāb aur saman
figs and grapes pleasant fruits are. Roses and lilies-of-the-valley

khūb-ṣūrat phūl hain. Kobī, ālū aur nāshpātī bāgh ke
beautiful flowers are. Cabbages, potatoes and pears garden

nabātāt hain. Sab darakhton se balūt aur ṣanaubar bahut
vegetables are. All trees of, the oak and the pine most

kām men āte[2] hain.
work in coming are.

[1]*There* understood. [2]Useful.

3.

(Vocabularies 7—10, pages 21—26.)*

Badan kī barī 'ujūba bandish hai. Chihre par
The body of very wonderful structure is. The face in

ānkh, nāk, gāl, munh honth abrū aur kān hain. Mard
eyes, nose, cheek, mouth, lips, eyebrows and ears are. Man

ke sir par aur munh par bāl hote hain[1] Ūnglī par
of the head upon and face upon hairs become-are. Finger upon

nākhun hote hain. Larkon ke mā bāp ko dekhā hai?[2]
nails become-are. The children of mother, father, I have seen.

Merī bībī aur betī Inglisiān men hain. Larkon ko chāhiye[3]
My wife and daughter England in are. Children should

ki wālidain[4] kā hukm mānen. Wuh gharīb 'aurat langrī hai.
parents obey. That poor woman a cripple is.

Merī topī, kurtī aur chhātā mujh-ko lā do Yih patlūn
My hat, coat and umbrella me (to) bring and give. These trousers

bahut lambī hai. Hāzirī taiyār hai? Kab taiyār karoge?[5]
toe long are. Breakfast ready is? When ready shall you make?

Taiyār hai ṣāhib mez par rotī, makkhan, kahwa, ande, aur
Ready is, sir, table upon bread, butter, coffee, eggs, and

sū'ar kā namkīn gosht[6] pāiyegā.
pig of salt flesh you will find.

[1]Grow. [2]Have you seen? [3]Should, or must. [4]*Their* understood. [5]Shall you have it? [6]Bacon.

* See "Hindūstānī Self-Taught.

Hamāre pās[1] *ko'ī chhūrī aur kāṇṭā nahīṇ.*[2] *Mujh ko piyāla*
Me near knife and fork not. Me (to) a cup,
tashtarī aur chamcha lā do. Mihmān-khāne meṇ ārām kī
saucer and a spoon bring. Drawing-room in ease of
chaukī,[3] *kauch, mez, gharī taṣwīreṇ aur ā'īna hai. Yih*
chairs, sofa, table, clock, pictures and mirrors are. This
ṣandūkcha aur sham'adān merī sone kī kothrī[4] *meṇ le-jāo.*[5]
box and candlestick my sleeping room in take-go.
Mere bichhaune par ek kamlī ḍālo.[6] *Diyā-salā'īyāṇ kahāṇ*
My bed upon a blanket throw. The matches where
hain? Maiṇ chirāgh jalānā chāhtā hūṇ. Is khet kā, aur
are? I the lamp to burn[7] desirous am.[8] This field and
mazra 'kā mālik kaun hai? Yih 'imārat kyā hai? Maḥṣūl-
farm of owner who is? This building what is? A custom-
khāna yā ḍāk-ghar? Yih rāstā kahāṇ ko jātā hai?[9]
house or post-office? This high road where to goes?
Mujh ko makbara kahāṇ mil-sakegā?[10] *Is sarak par ek*
I the cemetery where find able? This street in a
masjid, ek mandir aur ek shifā-khāna hai.[11] *Is shahr meṇ*
mosque, temple and hospital are. This town in
ko'ī maktab yā madrasa hai?[12]
a school or a university is?

[1]Literally = to me; verb *have* understood. [2]*Ko'ī nahīṇ* = no. [3]Easy-chairs. [4]Bedroom. [5]Take away [6]Put. [7]To light. [8]I want. [9]Does lead. [10]Can I find. [11],[12]*There* understood.

5.

(See Vocabularies, 14—16, pages 32—35.)

Mistrī barhaī ko aur rāzoṇ ko kām detā hai.[1] *Sāhūkār*
An architect to carpenters and to masons work gives. The banker
ke nawīsanda ne[2] *Pādrī ṣāḥib kī ustānī ko aur bāwarchī*
of the clerk, the clergyman of governess and cook
ko rūpiya adā kiyā.[3] *Kitāb-farosh kī dūkān meṇ bahut kitābeṇ*
payment made. The bookseller of shop in many books
hain?[4] *Is gānw meṇ koi ḥakīm yā dā'ī hai?*[5] *Munshī*
are. This village in any doctor or a nurse is(there)? The teacher
sikhātā hai aur ṭālibu-l-'ilm sīkhtā hai. Is jahāz meṇ bahut
instructs and the student learns. This ship in many
labūse hain?[6] *Hamāre daryā-i-safar meṇ ko'ī roshnī ke mīnār*
cabins are(there)? Our voyage in any lighthouse

[1]Employs. [2]Signifies agency. [3]Paid. [4],[5]*There* understood.

See "Hindūstānī Self-Taught."

dekhenge? *Nāo meṇ chau-taggī aur rassī rakh do.**
shall we see? The boat in fishing-line and rope (keep-give).
Ḥammāl mere asbāb ko lo, aur sarāe ke mālik se merā
Porter, my luggage take, and hotel proprietor from my
ḥisāb lāo. Is shahr meṇ ko'ī achchhī sarāe aur
account bring. This town in any good hotel and
tarjumān hai? Yahāṇ se rel-kā isteshan kitnī
interpreter are (there)? Here from the railway-station how
dūr hai? Khidmatgar! jo kuchh maiṇ ne adā kiyā hai us-kī
far is? Waiter, what payment I have made of that
rasīd mujhe lā do.
receipt to me bring.

*Place or put.

6.

(Vocabularies 17—20, pages 35—48.)*

Mujhe ḳalam, siyāhī aur kāghaz-i-jāzib lā do. Āp ke pās kuchh
To me pen, ink and blotting-paper bring. Thee near[1] any
likhne kā kāghaz aur lifāfe haiṇ? Apne dast-khatt yahāṇ
writing-paper and envelopes are? Your signature here
kījiye aur mujhe bhej dījiye. Yahāṇ ḳalam, aur
please write and to me send. Here a quill pen and
faulād-ke ḳalam haiṇ. In donoṇ meṇ se[2] kaun sā pasand
a steel pen are. These two in from which preference
karte ho?[3] A ṣāḥib ne mujhe parsoṇ ek tār kī khabar
make you? —Mr. to me day before yesterday a telegram
bhejī. Har roz maiṇ ṣubḥ-dam uṭhtā hūṇ aur ghurūb-i-āftāb
sent. Every day I daybreak rise and sunset
tak kām kartā hūṇ. Ek hafte meṇ sāt din haiṇ aur baras meṇ
till work do. A week in seven days are, and a year in
bāwan hafte haiṇ. Ā'inda[4] jum'a-rāt ko tum ko dekhne ko
fifty-two weeks are. Coming Friday you to see
āūngā. Baras meṇ chār mausim haiṇ: bahār, garmī,
I will come. The year in four seasons are: spring, summer,
khizān aur jāṛe.[5] Āp kī bandūḳ ke wāsṭe kuchh kārtūs haiṇ?[6]
autumn and winter. Your rifle for any cartridges are?
Merā kāṇṭā, chautaggī aur bansī kahāṇ haiṇ? Naddī
My fish-hook, line and rod, where are? The river
ke kināre ke pās bahut machhliyāṇ haiṇ?
of the bank near many fishes are?

[1]Thee near = have you? [2]Of these two. [3]Do you prefer? [4]Next.
[5]*Kā mausim* understood. [6]Have you?

* See "Hindūstānī Self-Taught."

7.

(Vocabularies 21—23, pages 43—45.)*

Āp 'adad-i-ẕātī aur 'adad-i-waṣfī bol sakte ho?[1] *Hāṉ jī.*
You the Cardinals and Ordinals speak able are? Yes, sir.
'Adad-i-ẕātī ek, do, tīn, waghaira haiṉ aur 'adad-i-waṣfī
Cardinals one, two, three, etc., are, and Ordinals
pahilā, dūsrā, tīsrā, waghaira haiṉ. Pachīs aur uske sāth
first, second, third, etc., are. Twenty-five and it with
das, pandrah aur pachās kyā ho jāte[2] *haiṉ? Ek sau. Is*
ten, fifteen, and fifty, what becomes? One hundred. This
paltan meṉ do hazār ādmī haiṉ. Har sāl rājah das
army in two thousand men are. Every year the prince ten
lākh rūpiye letā[3] *hai. Wuh imtiḥān kī fihrist meṉ ek-sau-*
lakhs rupees takes. He the examination of the list in one hundred
biswāṉ thā. Maiṉ ne paune-chār gaz mol liyā.[4] *Unhoṉ ne*
twentieth was. I a quarter-less-four yards price took. They
kal aṛhā'ī man ko'ilā kharīd kiyā.[5] *Is jagah*
yesterday two and a half maund coal purchase took. This place
se paune-pānch baje[6] *ham jāwenge.*[7] *Darbār meṉ*
from, a quarter-less-five have sounded, we will go. The Levée in
do sau biyālīs[8] *shakhṣ ḥāzir the. Maiṉ ne use āj*
two hundred forty-two men present were. I him to-day
do-bārā[9] *bāt-chīt kī.*[10] *Maiṉ ghar ko deṛh*
two-times conversation made. I to the house one and a half
baje phir āūṉgā.[11]
have sounded again will come.

[1]Can name. [2]Do make. [3]Receives. [4]Bought. [5]Purchased. [6]O'clock. [7]Shall leave. [8]*And* is never expressed with numerals. [9]Twice. [10]Spoke. [11]Will return.

8.

Maiṉ kināre par jānā chāhtā hūṉ, kitnā wakt[1] *lagegā?*
I ashore to go desirous am, what time will take?
Khidmatgār in ādmiyoṉ ko chukā do[2]*. Agar tum ziyāda*
—Butler, these men finish give. If you more
māṉgoge to maiṉ magistret se faryād karūṉgā. Tumko
demand then I to the magistrate complaint will make. To you
barābar ḥisāb rakhnā chāhiye.[3] *Jo kharch ho, so*
exact accounts to keep is necessary. Whatever expenses be, that

[1]How long. [2]Pay. [3]Must.

* See "Hindūstānī Self-Taught."

likho. Agar tumhāre pās achchhā kāghaz[4] *hai*[5] *main tumhārī*
write. If by you good paper is I you

āzmāish kartā hūn.[6] *Mujhe jaldī uthānā, aur garm pānī*
trial do am. Me early wake, and warm water

taiyār rakhnā.[7] *Main apne hāth se*[8] *hajāmat banānā*[9]
ready keep. I my hand with shaving make

pasand kartā hūn.[10] *Ustarā aur patpatī kahān hain?*
prefer make am. Razors and strop where are they?

Mere dagle par brush māro[11] *aur merī pāposhen dhūndho.*
My coat upon brush beat and my slippers search.

[4]Character. [5]Have. [6]Will give. [7]Have. [8]Myself. [9]Shave. [10]Would rather. [11]Brush.

9.

Ye kapre sāf nahīn[1] *balki bahut maile hain. Dhobī se*
These clothes clean not, but very dirty are. To the washer-

kaho ki agar wuh ziyāda mihnat na karegā to main
man say that if he more trouble not will do then I

use bartaraf karūngā. Hammālon ko pankhā sārī rāt
him discharge will make. The bearers the punkah all night

khainchnā chāhiye. Main sawārī par se ā'ūn us wakt
pull must. I ride from come that time

chāe kā piyāla lāo. Mujhe harī chāe nā-pasand hai, sab kālī
tea of cup bring. To me green tea not pleasing is, all black

rakho. Sab se achchhi zāt kī[2] *kaunsī machhliyān hain?*
keep. All from the best sort of which fish are?

Mere chand[3] *dost ānewāle hain, nāshta chār ke-wāste taiyār*
My several friends coming are, breakfast four for ready

karo. Mujhe shikār chāhiye.[4] *Āj rāt ko main bāhar khāne ko*
make. To me game desire. To-day night I out to dine

jānewālā hūn. Khabardār raho! merī kursī ke pīchhe
going am. Careful be! my chair of at the back

khare rahā karo[5] *jo mujhe chāhiye so dete raho.*[6]
stand keep do, whatever to me desire that giving keep.

[1]*Are* understood. [2]*Fish* understood. [3]*Of* understood. [4]I should like some game. [5]You stand. [6]Attend to my wants.

Maiṇ Kalkatte ko kal fajr jāūngā. Hukka pīnā[1]
I to Calcutta to-morrow morning will go. Hookah drinking

chhoṛo[2] *aur chalo. Tumhārī mem ṣāḥiba ghar meṇ hain?*
give up and go on. Your mistress house in is?

Nahīṇ ṣāḥib, darwāza band hai.[3] *Wilāyatī ādmiyoṇ kā banglā*
No, sir; the door shut is. European bungalow

yā kāle ādmiyoṇ kī[4] *sarā'e yahāṇ hāi? Is jagah meṇ sānp,*
or native's inn here is? This place in snakes,

bichchhū yā dūsre mūẓī kīṛe haiṇ. Tumko kyā hūā
scorpions, or other troublesome insects are. You what become

hai?[5] *Mere sir meṇ bahut dard hai; chakkar ātā hai.*[6]
is? My head in great pain is; giddiness coming is.

Apnī jībh batāo aur tumhārī nabẓ dekhūṇ.[7] *Tumko*
Your tongue show and your pulse I will see. To you

bhūkh[8] *lagtī hai?*[9] *Nahīṇ, jī, lekin piyās bahut lagtī*
hunger felt is? No, sir, but thirst great felt

hai.[10] *Is bastī meṇ ko'ī ḥakīm hai? Jo ho usē bulāo.*
is. This place in any doctor is? Whoever be, him call.

[1]To drink = to smoke (idiom). [2]Leave off. [3]She is not at home (idiom). [4]Native. [5]What is the matter with you? [6]Have. [7]Let me feel. [8]Appetite.

11.

Us shak̲h̲ṣ se kaho ki bāzū ho[1] *jāiye. Ghoṛā itnā*
That man tell that aside be must go. The horse so much

garm rahe[2] *to usko pānī na pilāo. Uske sum dekho*
hot keep then him water not give. His hoof look

shāyad ko'ī kankar yā patthar lag gayā hai.[3] *Ghoṛe kā*
perhaps some gravel or stone touch-gone is. Horse of

pāoṇ rāt kī rāt meṇ bahut sūj gayā[4]*; usko dekhne ko*
the leg night-time in very much swell-gone; him to see

na'lband ko bulāo. Pandrah āne baṭāwan, le-kar,[5] *mujhe*
a farrier call. Fifteen annas discount taking, to me

rūpīye do. Maiṇ tumko tīs din kī muddat kī huṇḍī
money give. I to you thirty days of draft of exchange

fulānī koṭhī par dūngā. Is kapṛe ke thān meṇ kitne
some bank upon will give. This cloth of piece in how many

[1]Out of the way. [2]Is. [3]Are sticking. [4]Has swelled. [5]After taking.

gaz hain? Āyah merī bībī ko hamesha fajr ke paune
yards are? Maid my wife always in the morning quarter less

chha baje[6] *uṭhāyā karnā.*[7] *Bachchoṇ ko har roz bilā*
six sounded wake up make. Children every day regu-

nāgha nahlāyā karo.[8] *Dāī ko bulāo, aur kaho ki*
larly wash make. The nurse call, and say that

dūdh pīte bachche[9] *ko letī āwe.*[10]
milk-drinking child taking come.

[6]O'clock. [7]Call. [8]Bathe. [9]Baby. [10]Bring.

12.

Merī zāuja, wuh peshwāz pahinegī jo darzī ne kal
My wife, that gown will wear which tailor yesterday

shām ko pūrī kī[1]*: taiyār kar-ke rakho*[2] *kyūṇki wuh jaldī*
evening finished: ready having done keep, because she early

jānewālī hai. Is bachche kā joṛā banāne ke
going out is. This child's suit of clothes making

liye nāp lo. Darzī yih peshwāz merī bībi ko bi'l-kul
for measure take. Tailor, this gown to my wife entirely

barābar ātī[3] *nahīṇ. Bārīk malmal aur resham ke tīn yā*
proper coming not. Fine muslin and of silk three or

chār thān is namūne ke dekhne ke wāsṭe kal lānā. Ek
four pieces this pattern of to look at to-morrow bring. A

bahut bārīk sū'ī lo, aur aisī be ma'lūm[4] *rafū karo. Jaldī*
very fine needle take, and so unobserved darn make. Quickly

karo! mujhe yih turt chāhiye. Is poshāk ko lambā karo[5]
make! I this directly want. This dress long make,

aur in kapṛoṇ ko durust karo.[6] *Wuh khilaune jo maiṇ ne*
and these clothes right make. Those playthings that by me

bachchoṇ ke wāsṭe kharīd kiye hain[7]*. so lāo. Kyūṇ! dāī*
for the children purchase done are, them bring. Well, nurse,

bachcha āj[8] *do-pahar ke āge soyā thā? Bachchoṇ ne*
the child to-day afternoon before slept has? The children

hanoz khānā khāyā?
yet dinner have eaten?

[1]Fem. past participle of *karnā*. [2]Have it. [3]Does fit. [4]It cannot be observed. [5]Lengthen. [6]Mend. [7]Bought. [8]This.

13.

(Vocabularies 28 & 29, pages 61—75.)*

Karnail ṣāḥib ne āj kyā ḥukm diye? Usne nāyak ko
The colonel to-day what orders has given? He to the corporal,
jamādār ko aur ḳil'adār ko ijāzat dī.
sergeant and warrant officer, leave of absence has given.
Gole bārūt kī gāṛī ko silāḥ khāne ko jaldī lāo. Risāle
The ammunition wagon to the arsenal quickly bring. Cavalry
ke wāsṭe taiyār ho aur ḳarnā'ī bajāo. Sipāhī ne gaye mahīne
for ready be,[1] and bugle sound. The soldier last month
apne fārigh ho jāne kī sanad lī. Jagah par khaṛe raho,
his certificate of discharge took. In place standing keep,[2]
dahine phiro, jaldī ḳadam uṭhāo. Kampanī kī chār ṭoliyāṇ
by the left turn[3] quick step lift up.[4] The company four sections
karo. Palṭan tirchhī ṭolī ho jāegī. Kampanī
make.[5] The battalion echelon of sections will be.[6] The company
chha ḳadam pīchhe haṭegī. Fajr ko kis waḳt
six paces back will step. In the morning at what time
palṭan kūch karegī?
the battalion march will make?[7]

[1]Prepare. [2]Fall in. [3]Left turn. [4]Quick march. [5]Tell off the company into four sections. [6]Will wheel in. [7]Will march.

14.

(Vocabulary 30, pages 75—76.)*

Inglistān tamām hindūstān ke sāth baṛī kharīd-farokht
England, whole India with, great trade
kartā hai. London ke baipārī bahut paise-wāle haiṇ. Is
does. London of the merchants very wealthy are. This
udhār ke-wāsṭe kyā biyāj māngte ho? Is milk ko kyā
loan for, what interest do you ask? This property upon, any
giro rakhā hai?[1] Jo paise maiṇ ne aur mere sharīk ne
mortgage kept is? What money I and my partner
koṭhī meṇ rakhe, so tamām ḍūb gaye. Is mulk se
in the bank kept,[2] that all[3] sink-gone.[4] This country from
bāhir jānewālā māl, aur uskī nikāsī bahut baṛī hai. Maiṇ ne
the export and the import very great are. I
āj-ke kāghaz meṇ ek ishtihār diyā hai. Wuh ḳarẓ-khwāh
of to-day in the paper an advertisement put. That creditor

[1]*There* understood. [2]Had. [3]The whole of that. [4]Has been lost.

* See "Hindūstānī Self-Taught."

apnā ḳarẓ be-muhlat māngtā hai. Us paise ke wāste,
his payment without delay demanding is.[5] That money for,
main tumko ek ruḳ'a dūngā. Har mahīne tum kyā tankhwāh
I to you an I.O.U. will give. Monthly, you what wages
māngte ho? Koshish men sustī na karo, rūḥānī josh men
do ask? In business slothful not make,[6] in spirit
bhare raho, khudāwand kī khidmat karte raho.
fervent keep,[7] the Lord service of[8] making keep.[9]

[5]Demands. [6][7]Be. [8][9]Serving.

15.

(Vocabulary 31, pages 77–78.)*

Khairāt denā, namāz parhnā, roza rakhnā ye tīn chīzen
—Alms to give, prayers to read, fasts to keep, these three things
Allāh ko pasand hain. Rūḥ kā ārām bihisht men hai; kharāb
God pleased is. Of the soul peace Heaven in is; wicked
ādmi'on kī sazā jahannam men hogī. Bhalā ādmī,
men of the punishment hell in will be. Good men,
gharīb logon ko khairāt degā. Ādmī kā dushman iblīs hai,
poor men to alms will give. Of man the enemy the devil is,
lekin uskā dost khudā hai. Mussalman logon ke dīn
but his friend God is. Of the Mohammedans the religious
kitāb ḳurān hai, aur hindū logon kī bhāgwat. Hindū
book the Koran is, and of the Hindus, the Bhagwat. Among
logon men chār aṣlī ẕāten hain:—Brāhman, Kshatri-
the Hindus four principal castes are:—The Brahmins, the Kshatri-
ya, Vaishya aur Sūdra. Islām men do firke
yahs, the Vyshya and the Sudrahs. In Islamism two sects
hain:— pahilā Shī'ah aur dūsrā Sunnī. Khudā
(there) are:—Firstly, the Shi'ah, and, secondly, the Sannis. —God
ne dunyā se aisī mahabbat rakhī, ki us ne apnā iklautā
the world so loved that He His only beloved
Betā bakhsh diyā, tāki jo ko'ī us par īmān lāe, halāk
Son freely gave, that whosoever him upon belief placed[1] dead
na ho, balki hamesha kī zindagī pāe. Gharaẓ īmān,
not be,[2] but everlasting life should get.[3] —In short, Faith,
ummed aur mahabbat, yih tīnon dāimī hain, magar in men
Hope, and Love, these three abideth, but in them[4]
mahabbat afẓal hai. Khudāwand Yisū par īmān lā,
love the greatest is. —The Lord Jesus on belief place;[5]
to tū aur terā gharānā najāt pāegā.
then thou and thy household shall be saved.

[1]Believeth in him. [2]Should not perish. [3]Have. [4]Of these. [5]Believe.

* See "Hindūstani Self-Taught."

16.

(Vocabulary 32, pages 76—85, "Hindustani Self-Taught.")

Yih 'adālat kab khulegī aur jaj ṣāḥib kaun hain?
This court when will open, and judge who is?
Faujdārī 'adālat das baje khultī hai, aur dīwānī 'adālat
The Criminal Court ten sounded opens, and the Civil Court
gyārah baje. Mudda'ī aur mudā 'alaihi kaun hain?
eleven sounded. Plaintiff and defendant who are?
Jaj ṣāḥib ne ḳaidī ko jhūṭhī ḳasam ke wāsṭe, chha mahīne
The judge the prisoner, for perjury, six months
ke liye ḳaid-khāne ko bhejā. Jallād ne Gopāl ko phānsi dī,
to prison sent. The executioner Gopal noose gave;[1]
uskā ṣubūt-i-gunāh inṣāfan thā. Sab gunāh se, jhūṭhī dastāwez
his conviction just was. All crimes from, forgery
banānā bahut kharāb hai: 'adālat men is wāsṭe jaj bhārī
very bad is; in court for it judges heavy
sazā de-dete hain. Uske muḳaddame men 'Alī Khān uskā vakīl
sentences give. His trial at, Ali Khan his counsel
aur Dharamdās uskā shāhid thā. Tumhārā bayān ek ṭarfī
and Dharamdas his witness was. Your statement *ex parte*
hai; tumhāre pās kyā dalīl hai? Hindustān men rishwat
is; you near[2] what proof is?[3] India in bribe-
denā aur chorī bahut 'āmm hain. Hukmnāma kyā thā?
giving[4] and theft very common are. The decree what was?

[1]Hanged. [2][3]Near is = have. [4]Bribery.

GENERAL EXERCISES.

[These Exercises are arranged to illustrate the peculiarities of the Syntax and Idioms of the Hindūstānī Language, to which the student should give particular attention.]

17.

Jab pādshāh shahr ko āte tab gharīb logon ko bakhshish
Whenever the King to the city came, then poor people to gratuities
dete.[1] *Agar Gopāl ātā, to main usko ek in'ām detā.*[2] *Āj*
gave. If Gopal had come, I would have given him a reward. To-day
hamko ghoṛe par jānā hogā.[3] *Agar us ādmī kā bhā'ī*
I upon a horse[4] go must. If that man's brother

[1]The verb is made plural, out of respect to the word *pādshāh*. [2]The *consequence* is also thrown into the same tense as the first clause. [3]Verbal noun followed by the infinitive. [4]On horseback.

āwe, *to bolo, ki* darwāza band hai.[5] *Wuh* apnā
should come, then say that door shut is. He his (own)

ghoṛā[6] *chāhtā hai; usko jaldī lāo. Main ne apne wāste*
horse wishing is; him quickly bring. I myself for

bahut koshish kī.[7] *Jo*[8] *ādmī ghar ke andar hai, uske*
many attempts made. What man the house in is, him

bulāo. Jaisā[9] *bāp, taisā beṭā. Kuchh parwā nahīn*[10]
call. As the father (is) so the son (is). Any care not

ek ek[11] *ādmī ko bakhshish do. Chirāgh ke niche andhera.*[12]
one-one man gratuity give. The lamp under, darkness.

[5]Idiom for "not at home." [6]His *own* horse. [7]Feminine past participle of *karnā*. [8]Relative pronoun is put *before* the noun to which it relates. [9]*Jaisā* ... *waisā* are used correlatively. [10]It does not matter. [11]Distribution is marked by *doubling* the numeral. [12]*Is* understood. This is an Eastern proverb.

18.

Tumhāre liye[1] *main āj āyā hūn. Gāṛiān wahān thīn aur*
Your sake I to-day come am. Carriages there were, and

ghoṛe bhī[2] *the. Darmiyān rāh ke, ek naddī milī*[3] *thī*[4].
horses also were. In the midst of the road one river found.

Rāh men ham do ādmion ko mile the, ek pārsī aur
In the road I two men came across; one Parsee, and

dusrā hindū. Us se pūchhiye,[5] *āj rāt ko kahān jātā hai.*
the second Hindu. From him ask to-night where going is.

Das barson se main ne apnā waṭan nahīn[6] *dekhā.*
Ten years from, I my own native country not seen.

Aktober mahīne kī das tārīkh ko[7] *Madras jāūngā. Merī*
October month of, ten date, Madras will go. My

ghaṛī bigaṛ ga'ī wuh kuchh kām kī[8] *nahīn hai.*
watch out of order gone, that some of work not is,

Smith ṣāḥib ko pahchānte ho? wuh bahut achchhe[9] *ādmī hain.*
Smith, Mr., you know? he very good man is.

Wuh bolā ki main Inglistān ko thoṛe dinon men jāūngā.[10]
He said that I to England few days in will go.

[1]When a word is itself a Genitive the Preposition follows it closely, without *ke* or *kī*. [2]*Bhī* is added to emphasise. [3]Is used most frequently as a third-personal verb only. [4]The verb is feminine, agreeing with *naddī*. [5]*Pūchhnā* takes *se* where we use *to*. [6]When *since* = "that I have not," a negative must be used. [7]In naming a date *ko* is used. [8]Agreeing with *ghaṛī*. [9]Words doubled to strengthen the force. [10]In narration the same pronouns and verbs must be used as those used by the original speaker.

19.

Āj kaun tārīkh hai? Āj Novembar mahīne kī nau
To-day what date is? To-day November month of, nine

tārīkh hai. Ḥuzūr kab tashrīf lā'e[1] haiṇ? Ek
date is. Your honour, when your presence bring are? One
hafta ho gayā. Ḥuzūr kab tashrīf le-jāenge?[2]
week been-gone. Your honour, when your presence take-away?
Agle mahīne meṇ. Hamko kuchh ummed nahīṇ hai[3] ki wuh
Coming month in. I some hope not is that he
jaldī achchhā ho jāwegā. Āj shām ko bāhar jāūṇgā ka'ī
quickly well will be. This evening out will go, what
baje[4] maiṇ ab nahīṇ jāntā hūṇ. Āp kā mizāj-i-sharīf[5]
sounded I now not knowing am. Thy health, noble,
kaisā hai? Shukr khudā hai.[6] Numā'ish aur ārā'ish
how is? Thanks of God is. Appearance and ornamen-
kī chīzeṇ zindagānī kī aṣlī ẓarūratoṇ meṇ kām
tation of things life of real necessities in use
nahīṇ ātīṇ.[7] Yih karo, jis ṭaraḥ ban paṛe.
not come. This do, in whatever way may be practicable.

[1] [2] *Tashrīf lānā* and *tashrīf lejānā* are used to native gentlemen of rank. *Tashrīf* = "the honour of your presence." In such case the verb must be in the third person plural. [3] "To have" is always rendered by "to be." [4] *Ka'i baje* = "at what time." [5] *Mizāj sharīf* is the polite form of asking a person's health. [6] *I am we l* understood. [7] *ātīn* = *ātī haiṇ*.

20.

Ādmī jo wa'da kartā hai, kamtar usko pūrā kartā hai.
Man what promise makes seldom it finish makes.
Ab chup raho, ek lafẓ bhī mat bolo. Tum koī dost rakhte ho
Now quiet keep, one word also not say. You some friend keep
jo tumhārā ẓāmin ho. Maiṇ ma'mūl se ziyāda denewālā
who your bail be. I tariff from more giver
nahīṇ. Wuh mujh se ek bāt kahtā hai, aur tum kuchh aur
not. He from me one word saying is, and you some more
hī kahte ho. Āp Hindūstānī zabān mushkil samajhte
still saying are. You Hindustani language difficult think?
hain? Jo tum itnā jald bolte to maiṇ tumhārī bāt samajh
If you so quickly speak, then I your talk know
nahīṇ saktā. Mutāla'a karne ko kaunsā waqt achchhā hai?
not able. Study making, which time good is?
Sawere. Mashk ke siwā, tum ṭarrārī se bol nahīṇ sakoge.
Morning. Practice without, you fluently speak not be able.
Farmāiye[1] jī iskā sabab kyā hai? Wuh bahut kharāb
Please say, sir, of this meaning, what is? He very bad
likhtā hai; uskā khaṭṭ ko'ī paṛh nahīṇ saktā.
writes; his letter anyone read not be able.

[1] Respectful Imperative form.

HISTORY. (*Tārīkh.*)*

[The following Reading Exercises are framed on the History, Geography, and Religions of India, the English translations being given on pages 62 to 64.]

I.

1. *Hindūstān kā ḳadīm nām jambudwīp thā.*
2. *Ḳadīm Hindūstān meṇ chha bādshāhiyāṇ thīṇ.*
3. *Uttar meṇ audh, hastināpura, magadh, aur mālwā the.*
4. *Mālwā kā bādshāh Vikram thā, wuh shāhzāda munṣif aur 'ālim ādmī thā.*
5. *Dakhan meṇ pāndyā aur cholā bādshāhiyāṇ thīṇ, inkā bādshāh Sālivāhan thā.*
6. *Musalmānoṇ ke shāhī-khāndān i.s. 1001 se 1744 tak the.*

II.

1. *Hindūstān kā pahilā ḳaiṣar Mahmūd-i-Ghaznavī thā.*
2. *Lodī kā rāj ḳarīb-ḳarīb assī baras Hindūstān kī ḥukūmat par jabr aur be-rāḥmī se rahā. Yih log Afghāṇ des se āye the.*
3. *I.s. 1526 meṇ Bābar Hindūstān kā pahilā baṛā Mogul shāhanshāh mushtahar hūā.*
4. *Shershāh ek afghān sardār ne Hindustān kī ḥukūmat baṛī ḳābiliyyat se kī aur usne mulk ke wāsṭe bahut achchhe kām kiye.*
5. *Ḳaiṣar Akbar sab Hindūstān ke musalmān ḳaiṣaroṇ se achchhā thā.*
6. *Akbar ke pīchhe uskā beṭā Salīm hūā aur usne Jahāngīr kā khiṭāb liyā.*

III.

1. *Ḳaiṣar Aurangzeb sab Hindūstān ke ḳaiṣaroṇ se ḥīlahbāz aur nāmwar thā.*
2. *Uskī ḥukūmat meṇ Mogul kī bādshāhī kī ḳudrat aur jalāl bahut baṛā ho gayā thā.*
3. *Marhaṭṭe logoṇ kī ḥukūmat kī bunyād Sivājī ne ḍālī.*
4. *Hindūstān meṇ jo pahile Yurup ke log ākar base wuh Purtagīz the.*
5. *I.s. 1600 meṇ Angrez log malika Elizabath se sanad ḥāṣil karke mashraḳī Hind se tijārat karne lage.*
6. *Us waḳt se Hindūstān, ziyāda yā kam, Angrez kī ḥukūmat meṇ rahā hai.*

---

* **History of India, published by the Vernacular Press, Bombay.**

GEOGRAPHY. (*Jughrāfiya.*)*

I.

1. *Rās Kāmrin se Panjāb tak, Hindūstān kī lambāī ek hazār āṭh sau mīl hai.*
2. *Karāchī se pūrab Bangāl tak Hindūstān kī chauṛāī pandrah sau mīl hai.*
3. *Hindūstān meṇ ḳarīb-ḳarīb tīn karoṛ ādmī haiṇ.*
4. *Vindhyā pahāṛ Hindūstān ko do baṛe ḥiṣṣoṇ meṇ taḳsīm kartā hai.*
5. *Hindūstān kī aṣl naddiyāṇ gangā aur indrā haiṇ.*
6. *Hindūstān ke uttar meṅ himālaya pahāṛ hai.*

II.

1. *Himālaya pahāṛ kī bulandtarīn choṭiyāṇ dwalaghirī aur gaurīshankar haiṇ, aur ḳarīb-ḳarīb untīs hazār fīt har-ek ūṇchī hai.*
2. *Hindūstān ke dakhan meṇ lankā kā jazīra hai.*
3. *Hindūstān ki āb-o-hawā maidān meṇ bahut garm ma'lūm hotī hai.*
4. *Dhān, kelā, gannā, afyūn, nīl, rū'ī aur gond ye chīzeṇ Hindūstān kī paidāwār haiṇ.*
5. *Barāmad kā aṣl asbāb, chāwal, rū'ī, chāe, aur resham haiṇ.*
6. *Darāmad kā aṣl asbāb wilāyatī dast-kāriyāṇ haiṇ.*

III.

1. *Hindūstān meṇ āṭh rel-ke-rāste haiṇ.*
2. *Gaikwār kā dārul-mulk Barodā hai.*
3. *Sūrat meṇ pahile angrezī tijārat khāne kī bunyād ḍālī gaī.*
4. *Hindūstān meṇ sab shahroṇ se Bumbai shahr bahut ābād hai.*
5. *Wilāyat se Bumbai ko pahuṇchne ke wāsṭe aṭhārah din lagte haiṇ.*
6. *Hindūstān kā dārul-ḥukūmat Kalkattā hai: yih shahr Hughlī naddī par hai.*

IV.

1. *Madrās ke zil'e kā dārul-ḥukūmat shahr Madrās hai.*
2. *Wilāyat se Madrās ko pahuṇchne ke wāsṭe bīs din aur Kalkatte ko ikkīs din lagte haiṇ.*

---

* Mackay's Geography Manual.

3. *Allahabad, Banaras, Tanjur, Amritsar, aur Punā Hindūstān ke mukaddas shahr hain.*
4. *Jab Akbar kaiṣar thā tab Agrā Mogul bādshāhī kā pā-i-takht thā.*
5. *Hindūstān kā kadīm dārus-saltanat Dehlī thā.*
6. *Merath men Hindūstān kī baghāwat bar-pā hūī, is liye yih jagah mashhūr hai.*

RELIGIONS. (*Dīn.*)*

I.

1. *Hindūstān ke pūjā-khāne Vishnu aur Shiva ke nām par hain.*
2. *Hindū logon kī dīnī kitābon ke nām Ved hain.*
3. *Hindūstān ke dūsre dīn Buddh dharm, Islām aur Zartushtī dharm, hain.*
4. *Buddh kā dharm karīb-karīb sāt hazār baras 'īsawī san ke āge mukarrar hūā thā.*
5. *Iske bānī kā nām Sākaya Munī.*
6. *Wuh Bahār ke ṣūbah kā sākin thā.*

II.

1. *Buddh ke dīn ke logon kā mukaddas makām Lassā hai. Yih jagah Tibat des men hai.*
2. *Dīn-i-Islām kī Muhammad ne bunyād ḍālī. Yih shakhṣ 'Arab des men paidā huā thā.*
3. *Dīn-i-Islām kī dīnī kitāb Kurān hai, aur 'Arabī zabān men hai.*
4. *Rūm kā Sultān is dīn kā khalīfa hai.*
5. *Musalmān logon kā mukaddas din jum'a hai.*
6. *Muhammad Makke men paidā hūe aur Madīne men wafāt pāī.*

III.

1. *Zartusht, Urimiah men paidā huā thā.*
2. *Uske dīn men, sūraj, chānd, āg aur pānī kī pūjā karte hain.*
3. *Hindūstān ke Pārsī log is dīn ke pairau hain.*
4. *Pārsī logon kā nām Irān men gabr hai.*
5. *Yih log Bumbai ko apnā des samajhte hain.*
6. *Pārsī logon kī zabān gujrātī hai lekin gujrātī zabān khūb nahīn.*

---

* E. B. Eastwick's (C. B.) "Religions of India."

HISTORY. [TRANSLATION.]

[This and two following Exercises are intended for re-translation into Hindūstāni.]

I.

1. The ancient name of India was Jambudvipa.
2. Ancient India consisted of six kingdoms.
3. In the north Oude, Hastinapura, Magadh, and Malwa.
4. The kingdom of Malwa was governed by Vikram, a just and learned prince.
5. In the South were the kingdoms of Pandya and Chola, which were governed by Salivahna A.D. 77.
6. The Mahomedan dynasties extended from A.D. 1001 to 1744.

II.

1. The first Mahomedan Emperor of India was Mahomed of Ghuzni.
2. The Lodi kings, an Afghan family, reigned about eighty years in a cruel, overbearing manner.
3. In A.D. 1526 Babar was proclaimed the first great Mogul Emperor of India.
4. Shirshah was an Afghan chief who governed India with great ability, and did a great deal of good for the country.
5. Akbar was the best of the Mahomedan Emperors of India.
6. He was succeeded by his son Selim, who assumed the title of Jehangir.

III.

1. The most crafty and ambitious Emperor of India was Aurungazib.
2. Under his rule the Mogul Empire reached the summit of its glory and power.
3. The founder of the Mahratta dynasty was Sivaji.
4. The first European settlers were the Portuguese.
5. In A.D. 1600 the English, under Queen Elizabeth, obtained a charter to trade with the East Indies.
6. Since that period India has been more or less under British rule.

GEOGRAPHY. [Translation.]

I.

1. The length of India, from Cape Comorin to the Punjab is 1,800 miles.
2. Its breadth, from Karachi to the East of Bengal, is 1,500 miles.
3. The population of India is about 290 millions.
4. India is divided into two large portions by the Vindhya mountains.
5. The principal rivers of India are the Ganges and the Indus.
6. The Himalayas are situated in the North of India.

II.

1. The highest peaks are Dwalaghiri and Everest, each nearly 29,000 feet in height.
2. The island of Ceylon is in the South of India.
3. The climate of India is excessively hot in the plains.
4. The productions of India are rice, bananas, sugar-cane, opium, indigo, cotton, and gum.
5. The principal exports are rice, cotton, tea, and silk.
6. The imports are chiefly articles of European manufacture.

III.

1. There are eight railways in India.
2. Baroda is the capital of the Gaikwar
3. In Surat the first mercantile establishment was founded.
4. Bombay is the most populous city in India.
5. It takes eighteen days to reach Bombay from England.
6. Calcutta, the capital of India, is on the river Hughli.

IV.

1. Madras is the capital of the Madras Presidency.
2. It takes twenty days to reach Madras, and twenty-one to Calcutta from England.

3. Allahabad, Benares, Tanjore, Amritsar, and Poona are sacred cities in India.
4. Agra was the capital of the Mogul Empire under Akbar.
5. Delhi was the ancient capital of India.
6. Meerut is famous for the Indian mutiny.

RELIGIONS. [Translation.]

I.

1. The temples of India are dedicated to Vishnu and Shiva.
2. The *Vedas* are the books which contain the religion of the Hindus.
3. The other religions of India are Buddhism, Islamism, and Zoroastrianism.
4. Buddhism was founded about 7,000 years before the Christian Era.
5. Its founder's name was Mani.
6. He was a native of the province of Behar.

II.

1. The sacred capital of the Buddhists is Lasa, in Thibet.
2. Islamism was founded by Mahomed, of Arabia.
3. The sacred book is the Koran, written in Arabic.
4. The Sultan of Turkey is the head of the church.
5. Their sacred day is Friday.
6. Mahomed was born at Mecca, and carried to Heaven at Medina.

III.

1. Zoroaster was born at Urimiah.
2. His religion chiefly venerates the sun, earth, fire, and water.
3. The Parsees of India belong to this religion.
4. In Persia they are known as the Guebres.
5. They regard Bombay as their native place.
6. Their language is a corrupted form of Guzerati.

Shiv and the Grasshopper.* BY RUDYARD KIPLING.

(*Shiva aur ṭiḍḍī.*)

Note.—A close rendering of the Poem is given in Hindūstāni, together with an *ad literatim* translation, in order that the student may note the peculiarities in the construction of the language.

(THE SONG THAT TOOMAI'S MOTHER SANG TO THE BABY.)
(*Jo gīt Tumai ki mā bachcha miyāṇ ko gāyā.*)
(Which the song of Tumai the mother to the baby sang.)

Shiv, who poured the harvest and made the winds to blow,
Shivane jo faṣl ke wāsṭe barsātā hai aur hawā ko chalātā hai
Shiv, who harvest for causes rain and winds makes to blow,

Sitting at the doorways of a day of long ago,
Bahut dinoṇ ke pahile, ek roz darwāza par baiṭh-kar-ke,
Many days ago, one day on the door having seated,

Gave to each his portion, food and toil and fate,
From the King upon the *guddee* to the Beggar at the gate.
Ek ek ko jo rājā gaddī par hai aur jo bhīkhārī dar-
One-one to who kings *guddee*[1] upon are and who beggars at
wāza ke pās bhīk māngtā hai [*diyā.*
the gate alms asking are [gave.
Unko harek kī khwurāk kā aur mihnat kā aur ḳismat kā ḥiṣṣa
(To them) his of food and toil and fate portion

All things made he—Shiva the Preserver.
Sab māl-o-matā' usne banāye—Shiva jahān-panāh.
All things he made—Shiva the Protector of the Universe.

Mahadeo! Mahadeo! he made all,—
Mahādeo! Mahādeo! usne sub banāye,—
Mahadeo![2] *Mahadeo!* he all created,—

Thorn for the camel, fodder for the kine,
Unṭ ke wāsṭe kānṭā, gāe ke wāsṭe ghās,
The camel for (the) thorn, the kine for (the) fodder,

And mother's heart for sleepy head, O little son of mine!
Aur nīndbhare sar ke wāsṭe mā kā dil, ai mere chhoṭe beṭe!
And sleepy head for of a mother the heart, O my little son!

[1]Throne. [2]The Great God.

---

* *The Jungle Book* (pages 244 and 245), by Rudyard Kipling. (1900. London: Macmillan & Co., Ltd.)

Wheat he gave to rich folk, millet to the poor,
Usne paisewālon ko gehūn aur gharīb logon ko bājrā diyā,
He to the wealthy wheat and to poor folk millet gave,

Broken scraps for holy men that beg from door to door;
Aur faḳīron ko jo dar dar bhīk māngte phirte hain
And mendicants who door (to) door (from) alms asking are
un-ko roṭi ke ṭukṛe diye;
to them fragments gave,

Cattle to the tiger, carrion to the kite,
Sher ko maweshī, aur chīl ko murdār gosht diyā,
To the tiger cattle, and to the kite dead flesh, gave,

And rags and bones to wicked wolves without the wall at night.
Aur bad bheṛiyon ko jo rāt ke waḳt dīwār ke bāhar ā jāte hain,
And wicked wolves who at night-time of the walls outside are,
un-ko bhī gūdaṛ aur haḍḍiyāṇ de dīn.
to them also rags and bones he gave.

Naught he found too lofty, none he saw too low—
Na kisī ko usne mustaghnī pāyā aur na kisī ko nā-
None he lofty found and none not
sazā dekhā—
low he saw—

Parbati beside him watched them come and go;
Pārbatī ne uske pās se un-ko āte jāte dekhā;
Parbati also near him (from) them coming and going saw;

Thought to cheat her husband, turning Shiv to jest—
Dil men sochā ki, apne khāwand se tamaskhur kare,
In heart thought that her husband to cheat (she) would be able,
aur Shiva ko aḥmaḳ banāe—
and Shiva fool make—

Stole the little grasshopper and hid it in her breast.
Ek chhoṭī tiḍḍī chorā-kar, usko apne chhātī men
A little grasshopper, stolen having, (and) it her own breast in
chhipā rakhī.
secretly kept.

So she tricked him, Shiva the Preserver.
Is taraḥ usne usko, ya'nī Shiva jahān-panāh,
In this manner she him, viz., Shiv the Protector of the Universe,
ko aḥmaḳ banāyā.
to fool made.

Mahadeo! Mahadeo! turn and see.
Mahādeo! Mahādeo! phiro aur dekho.
Mahadeo! *Mahadeo!* turn thou and look.

Tall are the camels, heavy are the kine,
Ūnṭ ūnche haiṇ; gā'en bhārī haiṇ,
Camels high are, kine heavy are,

But this was least of little things, O little son of mine!
Lekin yih sab chhoṭī chīzoṇ se chhoṭī thī, Ai mere chhoṭe beṭe!
But this of all little things (the) least was, O, my little son!

When the dole was ended, laughingly she said,
Jab ḳismat tamām ho chukī Pārbatī ne hans-kar kahā,
When the dole all was finished Parbati laughingly said,

'Master, of a million mouths is not one unfed?'
'*Ai! das lākh munh ke rozī-rasān, kyā koī bhūkhā nahīṇ*
'Oh! million mouths of provider, what none hungry not
rahā?'
is?'

Laughing, Shiv made answer, 'All have had their part,
Shiva ne hans-kar jawāb diyā, 'ki sab logoṇ ko apnā ḥiṣṣa
Shiv laughingly answer gave, that 'all their portions
mil gayā,
have had,

Even he, the little one, hidden 'neath thy heart.'
Us chhoṭī ṭiḍḍī ko bhī jo tumne apnī chhātī meṇ
That little grasshopper even which you your breast in
chhipā rakhī.'
secretly have kept.'

From her breast she plucked it, Parbati the thief,
Tab apnī chhātī se ṭiḍḍī ko nikāl liyā, Pārbatī
Then she her own breast from (the) grasshopper pulled out, Parbati
ne jo chor (thī).
who thief (was).

Saw the Least of Little Things gnawed a new-grown leaf!
Dekhā ki chhoṭī chīzoṇ se chhoṭī ne ek tāza pattā
Saw that little things from least a fresh leaf

toṛ-kar khā liyā!
having torn took and ate!

Saw and feared and wondered, making prayer to Shiv,
Pārbatī Shiva ko dekh-kar ḍar gayī aur mutaḥayyir
Parbati, Shiv having seen, became frightened and with wonder

ho-kar uskī pūjā karne lagī.
being filled to him supplications making began.

Who hath surely given meat to all that live.
Kyūṇki, Shiva ne, sabhon ko, jo jīte haiṇ, albatta
Because Shiv to all who alive are, certainly

khẉurāk dī.
food gave.

THE LORD'S PRAYER.*

(With Phonetic Pronunciation and an *ad literatim* translation.)

(Ḥazrat 'Īsā kī namāz.)

Hazrut eesah kee numahs.

THE GOSPEL OF MATTHEW, CHAPTER 6, VERSE 9, &c.

(Mattī kī injīl—bāb chha—āyat nau, waghaira.)

Muttee kee injeel—bahb chah—ahyut now, wughyrah.

(Matthew-of the Gospel, Chapter 6, Verse 9, etc.)

Our Father, which art in Heaven, hallowed be thy Name.
Ai hamāre bāp jo āsmān par hai, tere nām kī takdīs ho,
I humahray bahp jo ahsmahn pur hy, tayray nahm kee tukdees ho,
O our Father who heaven above is, Thy name holy be,

* See page 75.

Thy kingdom come. Thy will be done on earth, as it is
terī bādshāhat āwe, terī marzī jaisī āsmān par hai
tayree bahdshahhut ahway, tayree mursee jysee ahsmahn pur hy
Thy kingdom come, Thy will as heaven above is

in Heaven. Give us this day our daily bread. And for-
zamīn par bhī bar āwe, hamārī rozīne kī roṭī āj
zumeen pur bhee bur ahway, humahree roseenay kee rotee ahj
earth upon also fulfilled come, our daily bread to-day

give us our trespasses, as we forgive them that trespass
hamko bakhsh, aur jis ṭaraḥ ham apne ḳarazdāroṇ ko
humko buksh, our jis turah hum upnay kurusdahron ko
to us give free, and same manner we our debtors

against us. And lead us not into temptation; but
bakhshte haiṇ tū apne dain hamko bakhsh de aur hameṇ
bukshtay hyn too upnay dyn humko buksh day our humayn
forgive Thou our debts us forgive, and us

deliver us from evil: for thine is the kingdom, the
āzmāish meṇ na ḍāl balki burāī se bachā kyūṇki
ahzmahish mayn nah dahl bulkee burahi say buchah kioonkee
temptation in not throw, but evil from save. because

power and the glory, for ever and ever. Amen.
bādshāhat aur ḳudrat aur jalāl hamesha tere hī haiṇ.
bahdshahhut our kudrut our julahl humayshah tayray hee hyn.
kingdom and power and glory everlasting thine also are.

Āmīn.
Ahmeen.
Amen.

QUESTIONS IN HINDŪSTĀNĪ GRAMMAR.

(Or Specimens of Questions a Candidate for Examination is likely to be set.)

Elementary Paper.

A.

1. Name the dialects of which the Hindūstānī language consists, and by whom spoken.
2. Name the *Persi-Arabic* characters which never alter in form nor unite with the letter that follows.
3. How are the English Articles *a*, or *an*, and *the*, represented in Hindūstānī?
4. Decline the Nouns *bāp* (father) and *beṭī* (daughter).
5. What is the *simple* Accusative case, and when used? Give examples.
6. State clearly how to use the Particles *kā*, *ke*, and *kī*.
7. How many Genders are there? How are they generally distinguished?
8. How are Adjectives used, and when are they declinable and indeclinable? Give examples.
9. Give the rule for the agreement of Adjectives, and illustrate your answer.
10. Translate into Hindūstānī: (*a*) The man is tall, but the woman is short. (*b*) The woman's brother is wicked. (*c*) The man's daughter is good.

B.

1. What is understood by the term *Oblique* form of a Noun?
2. What is the effect of the Accusative in *ko*?
3. Give the rule for the formation of their Plurals, with examples.
4. Give the Gender of the following words :—*āg* (fire), *mez* (table), *dunyā* (the world), *pānī* (water), *motī* (pearl), *dahī* (curd).
5. Give examples of Adjectives used in making compound Verbs.

6. Illustrate by examples how to use the Genitive cases of Nouns and Pronouns.
7. How are sentences in Hindūstānī constructed when using the Verb *to be?* Illustrate your answer by an example.
8. How are Adjectives compared in Hindūstānī? Render in Hindūstānī :—(*a*) This man is taller than that woman. (*b*) This boy is the tallest.
9. Under what conditions do Verbs agree in Gender and Number with their Nominatives? Give examples.
10. Conjugate the Verb *to be* in the Past Tense, masculine and feminine. Translate: I will strike (m. and f.); I am striking (m. and f.); I was striking (m. and f.); I struck (m. and f.).

Intermediate Paper.

1. State clearly the difference between *Urdū* or *Rekhta* and the *Hindī*.
2. State the use of the word *āp* (self).
3. State the difference between the simple and compound tenses of Hindūstānī Verbs.
4. How are the compound Future Tense, Present Subjunctive, and the Imperative of English Verbs rendered in Hindūstānī?
5. Give all the component parts of a Verb.
6. Give in a tabular form the masculine terminations of Verbs (*Active*), Present Tense (Imper. and Subjunct.), Future Tense (Indic.), Present, Past, and Perfect Participles.
7. Show with an example how the compound tenses of *honā* are formed.
8. When by inflection two *a*'s or *a* and *e* meet, how are they are separated? Illustrate your answers.
9. State clearly how *must*, *ought*, *may*, and *can* should be rendered in Hindūstānī?
10. State how Verbs are intensified, and also show the peculiar usage of the Verb *chuknā*.

Advanced Paper.

1. How are Adverbs derived ? Show the peculiarities of Adverbs of time.

2. Give the irregular forms of the Imperative used by a a native in addressing his superior.

3. Give the Past Participles (masculine and feminine, singular and plural) of *jānā, karnā, denā, lenā, honā,* and *marnā.*

4. Give examples of masculine Postpositions with *ke* and feminine with *kī.*

5. What is the special use of the Participle in *ke* or *kar ?* Give an example.

6. Render into Hindūstānī : " He said he would go to Calcutta to-morrow," and state rule as regards narration.

7. How are Verbal Nouns of agency formed in Hindūstānī ?

8. State how to use the Particle *ne* in conjunction with an Active Transitive Verb.

9. Illustrate how the Passive Voice is formed.

Translate into Hindūstānī :—

10. Had I all along spoken the language of this country since I came, I should have been able to speak it now fluently.

11. I hear that you are well skilled in the Hindūstānī tongue.

12. The captain has given orders that the battalion will march to-morrow morning at six o'clock.

Translate into English :—

13. *Kitne din hū'e ki tumko yih khabar milī ?*

14. *Mushkil ho yā nahīṇ, miḥnat karne se, tum hamesha apne maṭlab ko pahūṇchoge.*

15. *Khānsāmān se kaho, pichhle mahīne kā ḥisāb taiyār kare.*

Part III.

THE VERNACULAR.

PHRASES OF DAILY LIFE AND IDIOMATIC SENTENCES IN URDŪ INTRODUCING MILITARY, LEGAL, AND COMMERCIAL TERMS, WITH THE ROMANIZED TRANS-LITERATION AND ENGLISH EQUIVALENTS.

ADVANCED READING LESSONS FROM CLASSICAL URDŪ WRITERS, AND A SET OF EXAMINATION PAPERS.

The student, who has now reached what may be regarded as an advanced stage in the language, should endeavour to master it in its *Native Form.*

Hitherto he has learned the tongue by means of Romanized characters, but to secure a complete and effective knowledge thereof it is very important he should be able to read and write it in the Vernacular.

To this end the Phrases, &c., on pages **76-85** will provide him with material for practice, as well as useful idiomatic Forms of Expression and Composition. On pages 8 to 13 (to which he is referred) the necessary assistance introductory to these Exercises will be found.

HINDŪSTĀNĪ PENMANSHIP.

At first sight one is apt to think that there is no difference between written and printed characters of the Persi-Arabic alphabet. But there is really considerable variation, and if a student will carefully examine the illustration of Urdū penmanship given on the opposite page, he will more readily realise the points of difference.

He should particularly note:

1. In manuscript the *short vowel signs* are generally omitted.
2. By the omission of the vowel *i* a final ی *y* may be read either as *ī* or *e*, the former being a feminine, the latter a masculine inflexion. In order to prevent this ambiguity of gender, a final *ī* is written ی, and a final *e* ے. This distinction is also observed in the printed character.. Thus, لڑکی *laṛkī*, 'a girl,' لڑکے *laṛke*, 'boys'; so also, کی *kī*, کے *ke*, سے *se*, نے *ne*, &c.
3. Instead of the four dots over the letters ٹ *ṭ*, ڈ *ḍ*, and ڑ *ṛ*, the mark ط, and sometimes -, is used, as لڑکا or لڑکا *laṛkā*, for لڑکا.
4. The initial combined form of ہ *h* is usually written ~ or ٦, instead of ھ; as, ہر or ہر *har*, 'each'; ہے or ہے *hai*, 'is.' So also the syllable *hā* is written ہا for ھا, as ہاتھ *hāth*, 'hand,' for ھاتھ.
5. The distinction between the medial 'butterfly' (or aspirate) form of *h*, i.e. ھ, and the second form ہ (as shown on p. 9) is not always observed, the form ہ being used for both. Thus, کہا may be read either as کھا *khā*, 'eat,' or کہا *kahā*, 'said.'
6. The final combined form of *h* is written thus, ہ, instead of the printed form ہ; as, نہ *nah*, 'not' (or *na*, the final *h* being omitted in transliteration: see p. 19); کہ *kih* (or *ki*), 'so that.'
7. With these exceptions, the letters are written very much the same as in the printed characters. In the 'Shikasta,' or cursive hand, many peculiar forms and combinations of letters occur which can only be learnt by practice. Letters which should not be connected with a following letter, as ا، ر، د and و, are generally written combined, and dots distinguishing the various letters are frequently omitted.

Urdū Penmanship.

— (The Lord's Prayer in Hindūstānī.) —

متی کی انجیل

باب ۶: ۹

اے ہمارے باپ جو آسمان پر ہے تیرے نام کی تقدیس ہو
تیری بادشاہت آوے۔ تیری مرضی جیسی آسمان پر ہے
زمین پر بھی بر آئے۔ ہماری روزینے کی روٹی آج ہمکو بخش
اور جس طرح ہم اپنے قرضداروں کو بخشتے ہیں تو اپنے دین ہمکو
بخش دے۔ اور ہمیں آزمایش میں نہ ڈال بلکہ برائی سے بچا
کیونکہ بادشاہت اور قدرت اور جلال ہمیشہ تیرے ہی ہیں آمین

— Numerals —

۱ ۲ ۳ ۴ ۵ ۶ ۷ ۸ ۹ ۱۰

PHRASES.

Though primarily intended for the study of the native characters, these phrases have been carefully selected for their practical bearing on daily life in India.

English.	Hindūstānī.	Romanized Form.
Have patience	صبر کرو	*ṣabr karo*
Keep quiet	چُپ رهو	*chup raho*
Get out of the way	هٹ جاؤ	*haṭ jāo*
Leave it alone	رهنے دو	*rahne do*
Get the bath ready	غُسل کا پاني تيار کرو	*ghusl kā pānī taiyār karo*
Get my horse ready	ميرا گهوڑا تيار کرو	*merā ghoṛā taiyār karo*
Enough! Go away	بس جاؤ	*bas! jāo*
Is the breakfast ready?	بڑي حاضري تيار هَے	*baṛī ḥāẓirī taiyār hai*
Shut the doors	دروازے کو بند کرو	*darwāze ko band karo*
Pull the punkah forcibly	پنکها زور سے کهينچو	*pankhā zor se khīncho*
Call the servants	نوکرون کو بُلاؤ	*naukaroṇ ko bulāo*
Where do you live?	تُم کهان رهتے هو	*tum kahāṇ rahte ho*
What is your name?	تُمهارا نام کيا هَے	*tumhārā nām kyā hai*
What is the difference between these two?	ان دونون مين کيا فرق هَے	*in donoṇ meṇ kyā farḳ hai*

English.	Hindûstânî.	Romanized Form.
The judge made a good investigation to-day	حاکم نے آج اچھي تجوِیز کِي هی	*ḥākim ne āj achchhī tajwīz kī hai*
What is your occupation?	تُمهارا دهندها کیا هی	*tumhārā dhandhā kyā hai*
What are you saying?	تُم کیا کهتے هو	*tum kyā kahte ho*
Are you fit for the business?	تُم اُس کام کے لایق هو	*tum us kām ke lāīḳ ho*
What sort of animal is this?	یهہ کونسا جانور هی	*yih kaunsā jānwar hai*
What is your advice?	تُمهاري کیا صلاح هی	*tumhārī kyā ṣalāḥ hai*
What crime has he committed?	اُس نے کیا تقصیر کي هی	*us ne kyā taḳṣīr kī hai*
Where did you hear this news?	تُم نے یهہ خبر کهان سُني	*tum ne yih khabar kahāṇ sunī*
Choose what is right and shun what is evil	حقّ بات اِختیار کرو اَور باطِل چهوڑو	*ḥaḳḳ bāt ikhtiyār karo aur bāṭil chhoṛo*
You are of no use to me	تُم میرے کُچهہ کام کے نهین	*tum mere kuchh kām ke nahīṇ*
Had I been you I should not have done it	اگر مَین تُمهاري جگهہ پر هوتا تو اَیسا نه کرتا	*agar maiṇ tumhārī jagah par hotā to aisā na kartā*
I waited for you till I was tired	مَین نے یهان تک تُمهاري راه دیکهي که تهک گیا	*maiṇ ne yahāṇ tak tumhārī rāh dekhī ki thak gayā*

English.	Hindūstānī.	Romanized Form.
You kept me waiting a long time yesterday	کل تم نے مجھکو بڑي راہ دِکھائي	*kal tum ne mujhko baṛī rāh dikhā'ī*
When I require you I will send for you	جب تمھارا کام پڑیگا تب بُلا بھیجُونگا	*jab tumhārā kām paṛegā tab bulā bhejūngā*
To persevere in a work is essential to success	استقامت سے هر ایك کام انجام پاتا هی	*istiḳāmat se har ek kām anjām pātā hai*
I am not pleased with him	مین اُس سے راضي نہین	*maiṇ us se rāẓī nahīṇ*
We can do without him	اُس کے بغیر کام چلیگا	*us ke baghair kām chalegā.*
How long will this examination last ?	یہہ اِمتِحان کَی دِن تك رهیگا	*yih imtiḥān kai din tak rahegā*
I will lodge a complaint against him	مَین اُس پر نالش کرُونگا	*maiṇ us par nālish karūngā*
Good men are scarce in the world, but bad men are plentiful	بھلے آدمِي دُنیا مین تھوڑے هَین پر بُرے بہُت هین	*bhale ādmī dunyā meṇ thoṛe haiṇ, par bure bahut haiṇ*
A friend in need is a friend indeed.	دوست وہ هَی جو بُرے وقت مین کام آوے	*dost wuh hai jo bure waḳt meṇ kām āwe.*
You are very lazy	تُم بڑے سُست هو	*tum baṛe sust ho*

English.	Hindūstānī.	Romanized Form.
Keep a civil tongue in your head	مُنھہ سنبھال کر بولو	*munh sambhāl kar bolo*
To what corps do you belong?	تُم کِس پلٹن مین هو	*tum kis palṭan meṇ ho*
Half cock your musket	اپنی بندوق کا گھوڑا ایك پاي پر چڑھاؤ	*apnī bandūḳ kā ghoṛā ek pāe par chaṛhāo*
The sepoys formed a square, fixed bayonets, and received the charge gallantly	سپاھیون نے کوٹ باندھ سنگین چڑھا بڑي بہادري سے حمله لیا	*sipāhiyoṇ ne koṭ bāndh sangīn chaṛhā, baṛī bahādurī se ḥamla liyā*
Obedience is the first principle of a soldier	سپاھي کے حق مین سب سے پہلا کام یہہ ھی که حُکم ماني	*sipāhī ke ḥaḳḳ meṇ sab se pahlā kām yih hai ki ḥukm māne*
In this engagement we lost 7 officers, 60 rank and file, 1 drummer, 7 *dūli-wālās*, and 9 camp-followers	اس لڑائي مین همارے سات عملدار ساٹھ سپاھي ایك پرگھمچي سات ڈولي والے اور نو آدمي بھیربنگا کے مارے گئے	*is laṛāī meṇ hamāre sāt 'amaldār, sāṭh sipāhī, ek parghamchī sāt ḍolī-wāle, aur nau ādmī bhīrbungā ke māre gaye.*
Your statements contradict themselves	تُمھاري ایك بات دُوسري بات کو جھُوٹھا کرتي هی	*tumhārī ek bāt dūsrī bāt ko jhūṭhā kartī hai*

English.	Hindūstānī.	Romanized Form.
Have you any suspicion against the prisoner ?	کیا تمھارا اس قیدي پر شبه هی	*kyā tumhārā is ḳaidī par shubha hai*
The laws of this country procure justice between man and man	اس مُلك کا قانون ایسا اچّھا هَی که لوگون کو داد مِلتِي هی	*is mulk kā ḳānūṇ aisā achchhā hai, ki logoṇ ko dād miltī hai*
How much per cent. interest do the bankers of this country give ?	اِس مُلك کے صرّاف في صدي کِتنے تکے بیاج دیتے هَین	*is mulk ke ṣarrāf fī ṣadī kitne ṭake byāj dete haiṇ*
At what rate of exchange did you get this bill ?	تُم نے اِس هُنڈِي کا هُنڈاون کیا دِیا	*tum ne is hunḍī kā hunḍāwan kyā diyā*
He is willing to allow 5 per cent. discount for ready cash	نقد پیَسا مِلے تو في صدي پانچ روپئے چھوڑ دینے پر وہ راضي هَی	*naḳd paisā mile to fī ṣadī pāṇch rūpaye chhoṛ dene par wuh rāẓī hai*
He drew on me one bill at sight and another at ten days' sight	اُس نے مُجھ پر ایك درشني هنڈِي لکھي اور ایك دس دِن کي مُدّت کِي	*us ne mujh par ek darshanī hunḍī likhī, aur ek das din kī muddat kī*
I drew a bill on Mr. ——, which he dishonoured	مین نے ایك هُنڈِي فُلان شخص پر لِکھِي تھِي سو اُس نے قبول نهین کي	*main ne ek hunḍī fulān shakhṣ par likhī thī, so us ne ḳabūl nahīṇ kī*

English.	Hindūstānī.	Romanized Form.
How far is the village from here?	گاون یہان سے کتني دور هے	*gāoṇ yahāṇ se kitnī dūr hai*
Sir, it is about six miles	صاحب کوئي تين کوس هوگا	*ṣāḥib, koī tīn kos hogā*
Am I following the right path, or is there some other road?	کیا مین درست راستے پر جا رها هون یا کوئي دوسرا راسته هے	*kyā, maiṇ durust rāste par jā rahā hūṇ, yā koī dūsrā rāsta hai*
No, sir, this is the road, but when you come to the peepal tree, then you should turn to the right	نهين صاحب راسته تو یهي هے لیکن جب آپ پیپل کے درخت تك پهنچين تو سیدهے هاته کو مڑ جائیگا	*nahīṇ, ṣāḥib, rāsta to yahī hai, lekin jab āp pīpal ke darakht tak pahuṇcheṇ, to sīdhe hāt ko muṛ jāiyegā*
The sky is cloudy: do you think it will rain?	آسمان پر گهٹا هے کیا تم سمجهتے هو که پاني برسیگا	*āsmān par ghaṭā hai: kyā, tum samajhte ho ki pānī barsegā*
Yes, sir, it is sure to rain, as the air is so still	هان صاحب ضرور برسیگا کیونکه هوا بالکل بند هے	*hāṇ, ṣāḥib, ẓarūr barsegā, kyoṇ ki hawā bil-kul band hai*
Will this rain do good to the crops?	کیا اس پاني سے زراعت کو فائده هوگا	*kyā, is pānī se zirā'at ko fāida hogā*
Yes, sir, a great deal of good	هان صاحب بهت فائده هوگا	*hāṇ, ṣāḥib, bahut fāida hogā*

EXTRACTS FROM CLASSICAL AUTHORS.

For Romanized transliterations of these extracts see pages 88 and 89, and for the English renderings see pages 89 to 91.

بیتال پچیسی *

شروع کہاني کا یہہ ہَی کِہ دھارانگر نام ایک
شہر تھا وھان کا راجا گندھربسین تھا اُس کِي
چار رانِیان تھِین * اُن سے چھہ بیٹے تھے -
ایک سے ایک بڑھکر پنڈِت اَور زورآور تھا *
قضاکار بعد چند روز کے وُہ راجا مر گیا اَور
اُس کِي جگہہ بڑا بیٹا شنک نام راجا هُوا * پھِر
کتنے دِنون کے پِیچھے اُس کا چھوٹا بھائي بِکرم
بڑے بھائي کو مارکر آپ راجا هُوا اَور بخوبِي
راج کرنے لگا * دِن بدِن اُس کا راج اَیسا
بڑھا کہ تمام جنبودیپ کا راجا هُوا اَور اچل
راج کرکے ساکا باندھا *

تب بیتال بولا کِہ اَي راجا بھوگوتي نام ایک

* "Twenty-five Tales of a Demon."

نگري هَی * وهان کا راجا رُوپسين - اَور چُوڑامن نام ايك طوطا اُس کے پاس هَی * ايك دِن اُس طوطے سے راجا نے پُوچها تُو کيا کيا جانتا هَي * تب سُوگا بولا کِه مهاراج مَين سب کُچه جانتا هُون . راجا نے کها جو تُو جانتا هَی تو بتلا کِه ميرے برابر سُندر نايکا کهان هَی * تب اُس طوطے نے کها مهاراج مگده ديس مين مگدهيشور نام راجا هَی اَور اُس کِي بيٹِي کا نام چندْراوتي - تُمهارِي شادي اُس کے ساته هوويگي * وُه اتِ سُندر هَی اَور بڑي پنڈِت .

پُورب کِي کهاني*

ايك آدمِي کے گهر مين ايك سَو رُوپِيے چوري سے گُم هو گئے تهے * اُس نے قاضي کو خبر دِي . قاضي نے سب نَوکرون کو طلب

* "Tales from the East."

کرکے ایک ایک آدمِي کو ایک لکڑي ناپ مین برابر دِي اور کہا کہِ جو آدمي چور هَے اُس کِي لکڑي ایک اُنگلِي بڑھ جایگِي * تب سبھون کو رُخصت دِي * رات کے وقت چور نے اَپنِي لکڑي سے ایک اُنگلِي کاٹ ڈالي * اِس طور سے قاضي نے چور پہچانا - اُس سے رُوپِیے لئے اَور سزا دِي *

نقل هَے کہ برسات کے مَوسِم مین ایک اُونٹ اَور ایک گدھا ساتھ سفر کو گئے تھے * درمِیان راہ کے اُنھون کو ایک ندي مِلي * پہلے اُونٹ پاني مین پیٹھا - گدھا کِنارے پر پِیچھے رہا - اُونٹ نے کہا ارے دوست کیون نہِین آتے ہو - پاني تھوڑا هَے * اُس نے جَواب دِیا البتّہ پاني صِرف تُمھارے پیٹ تک هَے لیکِن میرے کان تک ہوگا - مین ڈوب جاؤنگا - آگے جائیے مُجھکو معاف کِیجئے *

باغ و بہار*

اي ياران ميري پيدايش اَور وطن بزرگون کا ملکِ يمن هَي ۔ والد اِس عاجِز کا ملکُ التّجار خواجه احمد نام بڑا سوداگر تها ۔ اُس وقت مين کوئي مهاجن يا بيپارِي اُنکے برابر نه تها ۔ اکثر شهرون مين کوٹهيان اَور گماشتے خرِيد و فروخت کے واسطے مقرّر تهے اَور لاکهون روپيي نقد اَور جنس ملک ملک کي گهر مين موجود تهي ۔ اُنکے يهان دو لڑکے پيدا هُوئے ۔ ايک تو يهي فقير جو کفني سيلي پهنے هُوئے مرشدون کي حضوري مين حاضر اَور بولتا هَي ۔ دُوسري ايک بهن جس کو قبله‌گاه نے اَپنے جيتے جي اَور شهر کو سوداگر بچّے سے شادي کر دي تهي ۔ وه اَپني سسرال مين رهتي تهي ۔

* "Garden and Spring."

اي دلق‌پوشو يهہ عاجِز بادشاہ‌زادہ فارس کے مُلك کا ہَی * ہر فنّ کے آدمِي وہان پَيدا ہوتے ہَين - چُنانچِہ اصفہان نِصفِ جہان مشہور ہَی * ہفت اِقلِيم مين اُس اِقلِيم کے برابر کوئي ولايت نہِين - کہ وہان کا سِتارہ آفتاب ہَی اَور وہ ساتون کواکِب مين نَيِّرِ اَعظم ہَی * آب و ہوا وہان کي خُوش اور لوگ روشن طبع اَور صاحِب سلِيقہ ہوتے ہَين * ميرے قبلہ‌گاہ نے (جو بادشاہ اُس مُلك کے تھے) لڑکپن سے قاعدے اَور قانُون سُلطنت کے تربِيت کرنے کے واسطے بڑے دانا اُستاد ہر ايك علم اور کسب کے چُنکر ميرِي اتاليقي کے لِئے مقرّر کيے تھے - تَو تعليمِ کامِل ہر نوع کِي پاکر قابِل ہون *

PART IV.

KEY AND DICTIONARY.

TRANS-LITERATIONS AND ENGLISH TRANSLATIONS OF THE READING LESSONS,

ANSWERS TO EXAMINATION PAPERS

AND

CONCISE DICTIONARY

KEY TO EXTRACTS FROM URDU AUTHORS.

TRANSLITERATIONS.

BAITĀL PACHĪSĪ.

I.

Shurū' kahānī kā yih hai: ki Dhārānagar nām ek shahr thā wahāṇ kā rājā Gandharbsen thā, uskī chār rāniyāṇ thīṇ. Unse chha beṭe the, ek se ek baṛh-kar paṇḍit aur zorāwar thā. Ḳazākār ba'd chand roz ke wuh rājā mar gayā, aur uskī jagah baṛā beṭā Shank nām rājā hū‚ā. Phir kitne dinoṇ ke pīchhe uskā chhoṭā bhāī Bikram, baṛe bhāī ko mārkar, āp rājā hūā, aur bakhūbī rāj karne lagā. Din ba din uskā rāj aisā baṛhā ki tamām Jambūdwīp kā rājā hūā aur achal rāj karke sākā bāndhā.

II.

Tab Baitāl bolā ki Ai rājā! Bhogwatī nām ek nagarī hai, wahāṇ kā rājā Rūpsen hai, aur Chūṛāman nām ek ṭoṭā uske pās hai. Ek din us ṭoṭe se rājā ne pūchhā "tū kyā kyā jāntā hāi?" Tab sūgā bolā ki "Mahārāj! maiṇ sab kuchh jāntā hūṇ?" Rājā ne kahā "jo tū jāntā hai to batlā ki mere barābar sundar nāyakā kahāṇ hai?" Tab us ṭoṭe ne kahā "Mahārāj! Magadh des meṇ Mayadheshwar nām rājā hai, aur uskī beṭī kā nām Chandrāvatī hai; tumhārī shādī uske sāth howegī. Wuh ati sundar hai aur baṛī paṇḍit."

PŪRAB KĪ KAHĀNĪ.

I.

Ek ādmī ke ghar meṇ ek sau rūpiye, chorī se, gum ho ga‚e the. Usne ḳāẓī ko khabar dī. Ḳāẓī ne sab naukaroṇ ko ṭalab karke, ek ek ādmī ko ek lakṛī nāp meṇ barābar dī, aur kahā ki, "jo ādmī chor hai, uskī lakṛī ek uṇglī baṛh jāegī." Tab sabhoṇ ko rukhṣat dī. Rāt ke waḳt, chor ne apnī lakṛī se ek uṇglī kāṭ ḍālī. Is ṭaur se, ḳāẓī ne chor pahchānā, us se rūpiye liye, aur sazā dī.

II.

Naḳl hai ki barsāt ke mausim meṇ ek ūṇṭ aur ek gadhā sāth sāth safar ko ga‚e the. Darmiyān rāh ke, unhoṇ ko ek naddī milī. Pahle ūṇṭ pānī meṇ paiṭhā: gadhā kināre par pīchhe rahā. Ūnṭ ne kahā "Are! dost! kyūn nahīn āte ho? Pānī thoṛā hai." Usne jawāb diyā "Albatta pānī ṣirf tumhāre peṭ tak hai, lekin mere kān tak hogā, main ḍūb jāūngā; āge jā'iye, mujh ko mu'āf kījiye."

BAGH O BAHĀR.

I.

Ai yārān! merī paidāish aur waṭan buzurgon kā mulk i Yaman hai. Wālid is 'ājiz kā Maliku-t-tujjār Khwāja Aḥmad nām baṛā saudāgar thā. Us waḳt men koī mahājan yā baipārī unke barābar na thā. Akṣar shahron men koṭhiyān aur gumāshte kharīd o farokht ke wāsṭe muḳarrar the, aur lākhon rūpai naḳd aur jins mulk mulk kī ghar men maujūd thī. Unke yahān do laṛke paidā hūe. Ek to yihī faḳīr jo kafnī sailī pahne hūe murshidon kī ḥuzūrī men ḥāẓir, aur boltā hai. Dūsrī ek bahin, jis ko ḳiblah-gāh ne, apne jīte-jī, aur shahr ke saudāgar-bachche se shādī kar dī thī: wuh apnī susrāl men rahtī thī.

II.

Ai dalḳ-posho! Yih 'ājiz bādshāh-zāda Fārs ke mulk kā hai. Har fann ke ādmī wahān paidā hote hain, chunānchi "Isfahān niṣf i jahān mashhūr hai." Haft iḳlīm men us iḳlīm ke barābar ko'ī wilāyat nahīn hai wahān kā sitāra āftāb hai, aur wuh sāton kawākib men nayyir i a'ẓam hai. Āb o hawā wahān kī khush aur log roshan ṭaba' aur ṣāḥib i salīḳa hote hain. Mere ḳiblah-gāh ne (jo bādshāh us mulk ke the) laṛakpan se ḳā'ide aur ḳānūn salṭanat ke tarbiyat karne ke wāsṭe baṛe baṛe dānā ustād har ek 'ilm o kasab ke chunkar, merī atālīḳī ke liye muḳarrar kiye the, tāki tā'līm i kāmil har nau' kī pākar ḳābil hūn.

ENGLISH TRANSLATION.

BAITĀL PACHĪSĪ.

I.

The beginning of the story is this: that there was a city named Dhārānagar, the king of which was Gandharbsen, who had four queens, and by them six sons, each of whom was more learned and powerful than the other. It happened that, after some days, this king died, and his eldest son, who was named Shank, became king in his stead. Again, after some days, Bikram, his younger brother, having killed his elder brother (Shank), himself became king, and began to govern well. Day by day his dominion so increased that he became king of all India; and, having established his government firmly, he instituted an era.

II.

Then Baital spoke, saying: O King, there was a city, called Bhogwati, whose king was named Rupsen, and he had a parrot named Churāman. One day the king asked that parrot, "What dost thou know?" The parrot replied, "Great King, I know everything." The king said, "If thou knowest everything, tell me where there is a beautiful damsel, my equal in rank." The parrot said, "Great King, there is in the country of Magadh a king, Magadheshwar by name, and he has a daughter, whose name is Chandrāvātī. You will marry her: she is very very beautiful and very learned."

PURAB KĪ KAHĀNĪ.

I.

By theft a man lost from his house one hundred rupees. He informed the judge of the fact. The judge, having sent for all the servants, gave to each a stick of equal length, and then remarked as follows: "Whoever the thief is, his stick will increase by an inch." Then he dismissed them all. During the night the thief cut off an inch of his stick. Owing to this circumstance, the judge detected the thief, made him give up the money, and punished him.

II.

A story is told that in the rainy season a camel and an ass took a journey together. In the middle of the way they came to a river. The camel first entered the water, but the ass remained behind on the bank. The camel exclaimed, ' Oh, friend, why are you not coming? The water is shallow.' The ass replied, "Certainly the water only reaches your stomach, but it would cover my ears, and I should be drowned. Pray proceed along, and be pleased to forgive and excuse me."

BAGH O BAHĀR.

I.

Oh, my friends, the place of my birth and the country of my forefathers is the land of Yaman: the father of this wretch was Maliku-t-Tujjār, a great merchant named Khwājā Ahmad.

At that time no merchant or banker was equal to him. In most cities he had established factories and agents for the purchase and sale of goods, and in his warehouse were *lakhs* of rupees in cash and merchandise of different countries. He had two children born to him. One was this pilgrim, who clad in the *kafnī* and *sailī* is now in your presence and addressing you, holy guides. The other was a sister whom my father, during his lifetime, had married to a merchant's son of another city; she lived in the family of her father-in-law.

II.

O ye clothed in the *dulk*, this wretch is the prince of the kingdom of Persia: men skilled in every science are born there, for which reason the Persian proverb, viz., "Ispahan is half the world," has become well known. In the seven climes there is no kingdom equal to that ancient kingdom; the star of that country is the sun, and of all the seven constellations it is the greatest.

The climate of that region is delightful, and the inhabitants are of enlightened minds and refined in their manners. My father (who was the king of that country), in order to teach me the rules and lessons of government, made choice of very wise tutors in every art and science, and placed them over me for my instruction from my infancy. So having received complete instruction in every kind of knowledge, I am now learned.

ANSWERS.

Elementary Paper, A.

1. The dialects are two in number, viz.:—*Urdū* or *Rekhta* and *Hindī*. The former is principally spoken by the Mussulmans, and the latter by the Hindūs. (See page 7.)

2. The following are the *Persi-Arabic* letters which do not alter their forms with letters that follow them:—

   alif (a), *dāl* (d), *ḍa* (d), *re* (r),
   ṛa (r), *ze* (z), *zhe* (zh), *wāo* (w, *or* u).

   (See Alphabet, pages 8 and 9.)

3. As the Hindūstānī language has no Articles corresponding with that of English, the latter are rendered by the numeral *ek* (one) or by the indefinite Pronoun *ko'ī* (some, a certain), but when greater precision is required by *yih* (this) or *wuh* (that). (See page 14.)

4.

	Sing.	Plu.	Sing.	Plu.
Nom.	*bāp*	*bāp*	*beṭī*	*beṭiyān*
Gen.	*bāp-kā*	*bāpoṇ-kā*	— *-kā*	*beṭiyoṇ-kā*
Acc. & Dat.	*bāp-ko*	— *-ko*	— *-ko*	— *-ko*
Ablative	*bāp-se*	— *-se*	— *-se*	— *-se*
Locative	*bāp-meṇ*	— *-meṇ*	— *-meṇ*	— *-meṇ*
Vocative	*ai bāp*	*ai bāpo*	*ai beṭī*	*ai beṭiyo*
Agent	*bāp-ne*	*bāpoṇ-ne*	*beṭī-ne*	*beṭiyoṇ-ne.*

(See Declension of Nouns, page 14.)

5. The *Simple Accusative* case is the same as the Nominative, and is not formed with the Particle *ko*. It is used when the Noun is the *direct* object of the Verb, as:—*maiṇ-ne ek laṛkā mārā* (I beat a boy). (See page 15.)

6. The *Case* and *Gender* of the Noun regulate the selection. If Feminine, *kī* is used; if Masculine Singular, and Nominative or Simple Accusative, *kā* is used; and *ke* is used (i.) if Mas. Sing., and in any case *except* the Nominative or Simple Accusative, or (ii.) with Mas. Plural and any case in Plural. (See page 15.)

7. There are TWO genders, *Masculine* and *Feminine*. The latter Nouns in most cases end in *i*, *t*, *ṭ*, or *sh*, while the others may be regarded as masculine. (See page 17.)

8 Adjectives are employed in Hindūstānī the same as in English. They are only declinable when they end in *ā*.

E.g. :—*zorāwar ādmī* (a strong man),
achchhi beṭī (good daughter),
achchhe laṛke (good boys).

9. If the Noun be Masculine, *ā* of the Adjective remains unchanged in the Nominative and Simple Accusative Singular. It changes into *e* in all other cases of the Singular and in every case of the Plural.

Nom. & Simple Acc.
E.g. :—*achchhā ādmī* (a good man),
achchhe ādmī (good men),
achchhe ādmī kā (of a good man),

(See page 18.)

10. (a) *Mard lambā hai, magar 'aurat kotāh hai.*
(b) *'Aurat kā bhāī burā hai.*
(c) *Mard kī beṭī achchhī hai.*

Elementary Paper, B.

1. The *Oblique* form of a Noun is the slight modification which the original word undergoes before the Post-positions are added to indicate the particular case. (See page 15.)

2. Its effect is to particularise a special object.

3. The general rule for Oblique Plurals of all Nouns is :—All Nouns end in the Oblique Plural in *on̤*, and are formed by affixing this syllable to the Nominative Singular, or substituting it for the *e* (in those Nouns which have it) of the Nominative Plural, i.e., adding *on̤* to the inflexible (or radical) part of the word : *beṭā*, plu. *beṭon̤* ; *mard*, plu. *mardon̤*.

4. *Āg*, fem.; *mez*, fem; *dunyā*, fem.; *pānī*, mas.; *motī*, mas.; *dahī*, mas. The last three are exceptions to the general rule that words ending in *ī* are feminine. (See page 17.)

5. *Taiyār-karnā* (to prepare), *ḥāẓir-karnā* (to introduce), *ṣāf-karnā* (to clean). In short, by adding *-karnā* or *-denā* to certain Adjectives and Nouns, a large number of compound Verbs can be formed. (See page 34.)

6. *Ādmī kā ghar* (or *kuttā*), The man's house (or dog),
ādmī ke kutte ko, to the man's dog,
ādmī ke kutton ko, „ „ dogs.
ādmī kī mā, the man's mother,
ādmī kī mā ko, to the man's mother,
ādmī kī beṭiyoṇ ko, „ „ daughters.
merā bhāī, my brother,
merī bahin, „ sister,
tumhārā bhāī, your brother,
tumhāri bahin kā ghar, „ sister's house.
(See pages 15 and 23.)

7. The Nominative first, Accusative next, and the Verb the last of all:—

mard kī mā kahāṇ hai? Where is the man's mother?
yih merā ghoṛā hai. This is my horse.

8. The Comparative degree is formed by comparing the thing spoken of with *one thing* of the same kind, and the Superlative with *all conceivable things* of the same kind.

(a) *Yih mard us 'aurat se lambā hai.*
(b) *Yih laṛkā sab laṛkoṇ se lambā hai.*
(See page 19.)

9. In all the tenses except the Aorist and Imperative. (See page 27.)

Wuh 'aurat bakhshish māngtī hai. That woman is asking for a present.
Maiṇ ne bahut koshish kī hai. I have tried very hard

10. *Maiṇ* / *tū* / *wuh* } *thā* or *thī*, *ham* / *tum* / *we* } *the* or *thīṇ*.
(See page 28.)

I will strike,	*maiṇ mārūngā* or *mārūngī* (f.)
I am striking,	,, *mārtā hūṇ* or *mārtī hūṇ* ,,
I was striking,	,, *mārtā thā* or *mārtī thī* ,,
I struck,	,, *mārā* or *mārī* ,,

Intermediate Paper.

1. The *Urdū*, or *Rekhta*, abounds with words and phrases from the Persian and Arabic languages, while the *Hindī* consists of words of native origin, or words borrowed from the Sanskrit. (See page 7.)

2. The word *āp* ("self") is declinable. When used as a Possessive Adjective it becomes *apnā, apne, and apnī.*

   E.g. :—*maiṇ ap-nā ghoṛā ap-ne wāste chāhtā hūṇ.*
   I want my horse for myself.

   It is also used when speaking of or addressing a superior, and it is then equivalent to saying *your* or *his honour*, &c. (See page 23.)

3. SIMPLE TENSES are those in which no Auxiliary Verb is used to form them, while COMPOUND TENSES are made by the Present or Past Participle of the chief Verb *and an Auxiliary.* (See page 24.)

4. By the *Simple Tenses* in Hindūstānī. (See page 25.)

5. Every Verb consists of an invariable *stem* and a variable termination. Since the Infinitives always end in *nā*, the part of the word preceding it—even though it be a single letter—is termed its *stem*, and to which the terminations are added. (See page 25.)

6. Imp. & Subjunctive, Present Tense:

Imp. & Subjunctive, Present Tense:	*-ūṇ*,	*-eṇ*,
	-e,	*-o*,
	-e,	*-eṇ*.
Indicative, Future Tense:	*-ūngā*,	*-enge*,
	-egā,	*-oge*,
	-egā,	*-enge*.

D

Present Participle: *-tā.*
Past Participle: *-ā.*
Perfect Participle: *-ke, kar* or *karke.*
(See page 25.)

7. The compound tenses of *honā* are made with *honā* as the Auxiliary, the same as any other Verb:—

maiṇ hūā hūṇ,	I have been.
ham hūe the,	We had been.

(See page 28.)

8. When two *a*'s meet they are separated by the letter *y*, as: *ānā*, to come; *āyā*, came.

When *a* and *e* meet they are usually separated by *w*, as:—*ānā*, to come; *āwegā*, will come. (See page 26.)

9. *Must*, when used politely, is rendered by the word *chāhiye.*

Ought can be rendered by either *chāhiye, ẓarūr*, or *munāsib.*

May and *can* should be rendered by the Verb *saknā* (to be able) added to the "stem" of the principal Verb. (See Note 5, page 36.)

10. When one Verb is added to the "stem" of another it is then regarded as an *intensified* Verb.

E.g.:—*denā* + *denā* = *de-dena,* to give up.
pīnā + *jānā* = *pī-jānā,* to drink up.
kahnā + *denā* = *kah-denā,* to inform.

(See page 35.)

To *have done* or *finished* with a thing is rendered by *chuknā*, added to the "stem" of the principal Verb, as:—

wuh bol-chukā hai, he has finished speaking.

Again, the phrases "it's finished," "it's done," "it's all over," are rendered by *ho-chukā*, or its equivalent *ho-gayā.* (See Note 5, page 36.)

Advanced Paper.

1. The most useful Adverbs are derived from the five Pronouns *yih, wuh, kaun, jaun, taun.* A great number of Adjectives are also employed as Adverbs. The Adverbs of time are :—*kal* (to-morrow or yesterday), *parsoṇ* (the day after to-morrow, or the day before yesterday), *tarsoṇ* (the third day to come), and *narsoṇ* (the fourth day from this). (See pages 37 and 38.)

2. *Dījiye*, from *denā; kījiye*, from *karnā; lījiye*, from *lenā; pījiye*, from *pīnā;* and *hūjiye*, from *honā.* (See page 32.)

3.

	SINGULAR. M.	F.	PLURAL. M.	F.
jānā,	*gayā,*	*ga'ī;*	*ga'e,*	*ga'īṇ.*
karnā,	*kiyā,*	*kī;*	*kī'e,*	*kīṇ.*
denā,	*diyā,*	*dī;*	*dī'e,*	*dīṇ.*
lenā,	*liyā,*	*lī;*	*lī'e,*	*līṇ.*
honā,	*hū'ā,*	*hū'ī;*	*hū'e,*	*hū'īṇ.*
marnā,	*mū'ā,*	*mū'ī;*	*mū'e.*	*mū'īṇ.*

(See Verbs, page 26, and following.)

4. Masculine Postpositions with "*ke*":—
ke āge, before; *ke andar*, within.

Feminine Postpositions, with "*kī*":—
kī bābat, concerning; *kī jihat*, on account of.

(See Postpositions, page 22.)

5. The Participle in *ke* or *kar*, sometimes *karke* or *karkar*, all being derived from *karnā;* sometimes only the plain stem, *kar*, is used, to avoid the repetition of *and*, as :—

yih bāt bolkar chalā gayā.
Having said this, he went away. Or:
He said this much and left.

(See Foot-note, page 33.)

6. *Wuh bolā ki, maiṇ Ḳalkatte ko kal jāūṇgā.*

In narration the same Pronouns and Verbs as used by the original speaker must be employed. (See page 55, Exercise 18, Note 10.)

7. They are formed by changing *nā* of the Infinitive Verb into *ne*, and affixing *wālā* for the Masculine and *wālī* for the Feminine, as:—

likne-wālā, male writer;
likne-wālī, female writer.

(See Note 6, page 36.)

8. It is used when the Past Participle occurs and the the Verb itself (i.e., the Participle and Auxiliary) agrees in *gender* and *number* with its object, except when the latter is distinguished by the sign *ko*, in which case the Verb remains *impersonal* in the Masculine Singular. (See page 30.)

9. The Passive Voice is formed by prefixing the Past Participle of the Verb conjugated to the moods and tenses of *jānā*, to go, or be. (See page 32.) Examples:

The man is struck = the man is going struck = *mard pīṭā jātā hai.*

The horse will be beaten = the horse will go beaten = *ghoṛā pīṭā jā'egā.*

10. *Maiṇ jab se āyā hūṇ, tab se agar hamesha is mulk kī zabān boltā, to ab maiṇ bahūt ṯarrārī se boltā.*

11. *Maiṇ ne sunā hai ki tum Hindūstānī zabān se khūb māhir ho.*

12. *Kaptān ṣāḥib ne ḥukm diyā ki kal fajr chha baje palṭan kūch kare.*

13. How many days is it since you received this intelligence?

14. Be it difficult or not, by labour you will always arrive at your object.

15. Tell the steward to prepare last month's account.

ENGLISH & HINDŪSTĀNĪ DICTIONARY
OF EVERY-DAY WORDS.

ABBREVIATIONS.—*ad.* Adjective. *adv.* Adverb. *pl.* Plural. *pn.* Pronoun. *s.* Substantive. *v.* Verb.

English.	Hindūstānī.	English.	Hindūstānī.
Abandon, *v.*	*chhoṛ denā*	Africa	*afrīķa*
abide, *v.*	*rahnā*	after	*ba'd*
able	*ķābil, lā'iķ*	afterwards	*is ke ba'd*
ablution (before prayer)	*waẓū*	afternoon	*do pahar ke ba'd*
abolish	*mauķūf karnā*	again	*phir*
abominable	*makrūh*	against	*par*
abound	*bahut honā*	age	*'umr*
about	*ke pās*	agent	*nā'ib*
absent	*ghair-ḥāẓir*	agree, *v.*	*ķabūl karnā*
absolutely	*be-shak*	agreeable	*khush-gawār, maķbūl*
absurd	*be-hūdah*	aid	*madad*
abundance	*kaṣrat*	aim, *v.*	*nishāna lagānā*
abundant	*bahut*	alarm	*ḍarānā*
acceptable	*pasandīda*	alas!	*afsos!*
accompany, *v.*	*sāth jānā*	alike	*yaksān*
according	*ḥasb*	alive	*jītā, zinda*
account	*ḥisāb*	alone	*akelā*
,, (news)	*khabar*	also	*bhī*
accuse, *v.*	*nālish karnā*	ambassador	*safīr*
acquit, *v.*	*rihā'ī kar denā*	ambition	*ḥubb i jāh*
active,	*chālāk*	ambush	*kamīn-gāh*
adjust	*taṣfiya karnā*	ancestor	*jadd*
admiral	*amīrul baḥr*	ancient	*purānā*
admiration	*ta'ajjub*	anger	*ghuṣṣa*
admire, *v.*	*pasand karnā*	angry	*khafā*
adorn	*sajānā*	another	*aur ek*
advantage	*fā'ida*	ant	*chūṇṭī*
adventure	*khaṭre kā kām*	antiquities	*āṣār-i-ķadīma*
advice	*ṣalāḥ*	have you any antiquities?	*āp ke pās ko'ī purānī chīz hai?*
advise, *v.*	*ṣalāḥ denā*		
affair	*bāt*	anxiety	*fikr, andesha*
afraid, to be	*ḍarnā*	anxious	*mutafakkir*

English.	Hindustani.	English.	Hindustani.
any	*ko'ī, kuchh*	baggage	*asbāb*
anybody, one	*ko'ī*	bake, *v.*	*tanūr meṇ pa-*
appear	*ẓāhir honā* [*nā*	ball	*golī* [*kānā*
appoint, *v.*	*muḳarrar kar-*	banana	*kelā*
appointment	*kām, naukarī*	bandage	*paṭṭī* [*nā*
approach, *v.*	*nazdīk ānā*	banish, *v.*	*jilā waṭan kar-*
approve, *v.*	*pasand-karnā*	bank (river)	*pār*
Arab	*'arabī*	,, (money)	*koṭhī*
Arabia	*'arabistān*	bare, barefooted	*nangā, nange pāoṇ*
Arabic	*'arabī zabān*	bark (tree)	*chhāl*
Arabic (in)	*'arabī zabān*	,, (boat)	*chhoṭī nāo*
arch	*miḥrāb* [*meṇ*	barley	*jau*
arms (fire)	*sāmān-i-jang*	basin (for washing)	*bartan, bāsan*
around	*har ṭaraf*	bat (bird)	*chamgādaṛ*
arrange, *v.*	*band-o-bast kar-*	bath	*ghusl*
arrest, *v.*	*pakaṛnā* [*nā*	bathe, *s.*	*ghusl karnā*
arrival	*āmad*	bear, *v.*	*bardāsht karnā*
arrow	*tīr*	bear, *s.*	*rīchh*
art (science)	*'ilm*	bearer	*chaprāsī*
ashamed (to be)	*sharminda honā*	beautiful	*khūb-ṣūrat*
ashes	*rākh*	beauty	*khūb-ṣūratī*
asleep (to be)	*sote honā*	because	*kyūṇki*
ass	*gadhā*	beckon	*ishāre se bulānā*
assault, *s.*	*ḥamla*	become, *v.*	*ho jānā*
assembly	*jamā'at*	bed	*palang*
assist, *v.*	*madad denā*	bee	*zambūr*
assistance	*madad* [*nā*	beer	*bīr-sharāb*
astonish, *v.*	*mutaḥayyir kar-*	before (time)	*āge*
astonished	*mutaḥayyir*	beg (to)	*māngnā*
attempt, *v.*	*koshish karnā*	beg pardon	*mu'āf kījiye*
attendance	*ḥāẓirī*	beggar	*bhikārī*
authority	*ikhtiyār*	be gone!	*jāo!*
awful	*haul-nāk*	behind	*pīchhe*
awkward	*be-jā, mushkil*	bell	*ghanṭā*
Back, *s.*	*pīṭh*	belly	*peṭ*
back, *adv.*	*phir, pīchhe*	below, *prep.*	*nīche*
badness	*burāī*	bend, *v.*	*moṛnā*
bag	*thailī*	besides	*'alāwa*

English.	Hindūstānī.
between	*bīch*
beyond	*bāhar*
bill (amount)	*ḥisāb*
bind, *v.*	*bāndhnā*
birth	*janam*
bite, *v.*	*dānt se kāṭnā*
bitter	*kaṛwā*
blind	*andhā*
blood	*khūn, lahū*
blow, *s.*	*ẓarb*
blow, *v.*	*bahnā*
boar	*janglī sū'ar*
boatman	*mallāḥ*
boil, *v.*	*ubālnā*
bolt	*huṛkā*
book	*kitāb*
borrow, *v.*	*ḳarẓ lenā,* *'āriyat lenā*
bottle	*shīsha*
box	*ṣandūḳ*
brain	*maghz*
bracelet on the arm	*bangṛī*
bracelet on the foot	*pāzeb*
branch	*shākh*
brave	*dilāwar*
break, *v.*	*toṛnā*
breakfast (is) ready?	*ḥāẓirī taiyār hai?*
breast	*chhātī*
breath, *s.*	*dam*
breathe, *v.*	*sāns lenā*
bribe, *v.*	*rishwat denā*
bride	*dulhan*
brigand	*ḍakait*
bright	*raushan*
bring me	*mujhe lā do*
broad	*chauṛā*
broom	*jhāṛū*

English.	Hindūstānī.
brown	*bhūrā*
brush	*brush*
bug	*khaṭ-mal*
bull	*sānḍ*
burden	*bojhā*
burn, *v.*	*jalānā*
burst, *v.*	*phūṭnā*
bury, *v.*	*dafan karnā*
business	*kām*
busy	*mashghūl* [*tā hai*
buys (he)	*wuh kharīd kar-*
by-and-by	*ba tadrīj*
Cabbage	*kobī*
cabin	*jahāz kā kam-*
cage	*pinjrā* [*ra*
cake	*kulīcha*
call, *v.* (name)	*nām pukārnā*
,, (summon)	*bulānā*
called (it is)	*is kā nām*
called? (what is it)	*is kā nām kyā?*
camel driver	*shutur-bān*
can (I)	*main kar saktā*
cannot (I)	*main nahīn kar*
canal	*nahr* [*saktā*
candle (to light a)	*mom-battī jalā do*
canvas	*ṭāṭ*
capacity	*liyāḳat*
car	*gāṛī*
caravan	*kārwān*
care, *s.*	*fikr* [*wā nahīn*
care (I don't)	*mujhe kuchh par-*
careful	*khabardār*
careless	*ghāfil*
carriage (I want a)	*main gāṛī chāh-tā hūn*
,, closed	*band gāṛī*
,, open	*khulī gāṛī*

English.	Hindūstani.	English.	Hindūstani.
carrot	*gājar*	climb, *v.*	*chaṛhnā*
carry (to)	*uṭhānā*	clock	*ghaṛī*
cart	*gāṛī*	cloth	*kapṛā*
carve, *v.*	*kāṭnā*	clothe, *v.*	*kapṛe pahinnā*
cat	*billī*	cloud	*badlī, abr*
cataract	*pānī kī chādar*	coarse	*moṭā*
catch, *v.*	*pakaṛnā*	coast	*kināra*
cattle	*maweshī*	cock [café	*murgh*
celebrated	*nāmwar*	coffee shop,	*ḳahwa-khāna*
certain	*yaḳīn*	coins	*sikke*
certainly	*albatta*	cold, *ad.*	*ṭhanḍā*
chain	*zanjīr*	cold, *s.*	*sardī*
chamber	*kamra*	collector	*taḥsīldār*
change, *v.*	*badalnā*	college	*madrasa*
chalk	*khāryā-maṭṭī*	colour, *v.*	*rang denā*
charity	*khairāt*	column	*sutūn*
cheap	*sastā* [nā	come, *v.*	*ānā*
cheat, *v.*	*daghā-bāzī-kar-*	,, here	*idhar ā'o*
cheat, *s.*	*daghā-bāz*	,, up	*upar ā'o*
cheek	*gāl*	comfort	*tasallī*
cheerful	*khush*	comfortable	*ārām kā*
chemist (a)	*dawā-sāz*	command, *s.*	*ḥukm*
chemist's shop	*dawā-sāz kī dūkān*	,, *v.*	*ḥukm denā*
		commerce	*saudāgarī*
chess	*shatranj*	common	*'āmm*
chicken	*murghī*	compass	*ḳuṭb-numā*
chiefly	*khuṣūṣan*	compel, *v.*	*majbūr karnā*
choice	*pasand*	complaint	*nālish*
choose, *v.*	*pasand karnā*	complete	*kāmil*
christian	*kristān*	compliment	*salām*
circle	*dāira*	conceal, *v.*	*chhipānā* [nā
cistern	*kunḍ*	condemn	*nā-pasand kar-*
citadel	*ḳil'a*	condition	*ḥāl*
city	*shahr*	conduct, *s.*	*chāl chalan*
civil	*khalīḳ*	conscious	*mu'tarif*
civility	*akhlāḳ*	consul	*wakīl*
clean, *v.*	*ṣāf karnā* [rir	consulate	*wakīl-khāna*
clerk	*kirānī, muḥar-*	consult, *v.*	*mashwara kar-*
clever	*chālāk, hoshyār*	contempt	*ḥiḳārat* [nā
climate	*āb-o-hawā*	content	*khushnūd, rāẓī*

English.	Hindūstani.	English	Hindūstani.
continue, *v.*	*rahnā*	crown	*tāj*
contradict, *v.*	*khilāf kahnā*	cruel	*be-raḥm*
contrary, *ad.*	*khilāf*	cry, *s.*	*pukār*
convent	*dā'ira-i-zanān*	cure, *s.*	*'ilāj*
conversation	*bāt-chīt*	curtain	*parda*
cook, *v.*	*pakānā*	cushion	*gaddī*
,, *s.*	*bāwarchī*	custom house	*parmaṭ-ghar*
cooked	*pakāyā hū'ā*	cut, *v.*	*kāṭnā*
cool	*ṭhanḍā*	cymbals	*jhānjh*
copy, *v.*	*naḳl karnā*	cypher	*ṣifr*
cord	*rassī*		
corn	*anāj*	Dagger	*khanjar*
corner	*konā*	daily	*har roz*
corpse	*lāsh*	damage	*nuḳṣān*
correct, *v.*	*ṣaḥīḥ karnā*	damp	*gīlā*
cost(expense)	*dām, ḳīmat*	dance	*nāch*
cost ? (how much does it)	*iskī ḳīmat kyā ?*	dancing girls	*ṭawā'if*
		danger	*khaṭra*
costs (it)	*iskī ḳīmat*	dark, darkness	*andherā*
cotton tree	*kapās*		
counsel (advice)	*ṣalāḥ*	date (fruit)	*khajūr*
		,, (time)	*tārīkh*
count, *v.*	*ginnā, ḥisāb [karnā*	dawn of day	*baṛī fajr*
counting-house	*daftar-khāna*	dead	*mū'ā hū'ā*
		deaf	*bahrā*
country	*mulk*	dear(beloved)	*pyārā*
courage	*dilāwarī*	,, (costly)	*mahangā*
court (of justice)	*'adālat*	,, (it is too)	*wuh bahut mahangā hai*
courtesy	*akhlāḳ*	death	*maut*
courtyard	*ṣaḥn*	debt	*ḳarẓ*
cover	*ḍhaknā*	deceit	*fareb*
coward	*nāmard*	decide, *v.*	*ḳaṣd karnā*
creator	*khāliḳ*	deed	*kām*
creature	*makhlūḳ*	deep	*gahrā*
crime	*jurm*	defeat, *v.*	*shikast denā*
criminal	*mujrim*	defend, *v.*	*bachānā*
crocodile	*magar*	delay, *v.*	*der karnā*
crooked	*ṭeṛhā*	delight	*khushī*
crow	*kawwā*	demand	*māngnā*

English.	Hindūstānī.
denial	*inkār*
depart	*chalā jānā*
departure	*rawānagī*
depth	*gahrā'ī*
descend	*utarnā*
desert, *s.*	*bayābān*
„ (wilderness)	
deserve	*lā'iḳ*
desire, *v.*	*chāhnā*
despair	*be-ummedī*
despise, *v.*	*ḥaḳīr jānnā*
destroy	*nuḳṣān karnā*
devil	*shaiṭān*
devotee	*jogī, sanyāsī*
dew	*shabnam*
diamond	*almās, hīrā*
dictionary	*lughāt*
die, *v.*	*mar jānā*
difference	*farḳ*
different	*dūsrī ḳism kā*
difficult	*mushkil*
difficulty	*mushkilāt*
dig, *v.*	*khodnā*
directly	*fauran*
dirty	*mailā*
disease	*rog, bīmārī*
disguise	*bhes badalnā*
dishonest	*be-īmān*
dismiss, *v.*	*rukhṣat denā*
disorder	*be-tartībī*
dispute	*takrār*
distance	*dūrī*
distant	*dūr*
distress	*taklīf*
disturbance (riot)	*ghulghadr*
ditch	*nālā*
divide, *v.*	*ḥiṣṣa karnā*
dividend	*bakhrā*

English.	Hindūstānī.
do (to)	*karnā*
do it so	*aisā karo*
doctor	*ḥakīm*
doubt	*shakk*
doubtless	*be-shakk*
down	*nīche*
dragoman	*mutarjim*
draw (pull)	*khainchnā*
drawers	*pāejāma*
dream, *s.*	*khwāb*
„ *v.*	*khwāb dekhnā*
dress, *s.*	*kapṛe*
„ *v.*	*kapṛe pahinnā*
drink, *v.*	*pīnā*
„ *s.*	*sharāb*
drive, *v.*	*hāṅknā*
drop, *s.*	*ḳaṭra*
dromedary	*sāṅḍnī*
drown, *v.*	*ḍūbnā*
drum	*ḍhol*
drunk	*matwālā*
dry	*sūkhā*
dumb	*gūngā*
durable	*pāedār*
dust	*gard, khāk*
duty	*kām*
„ (tax)	*maḥṣūl*
dwelling	*makān, ghar*
dye, *v.*	*rang denā*
dyer	*rangrez*
Each	*har ek*
eagle	*'uḳāb*
earrings	*bālā*
early	*sawere*
earnest	*shauḳīn*
earth	*dunyā*
easily	*āsānī se*
east	*pūrab*
easy	*āsān*

English.	Hindūstani.
eat, *v.*	*khānā*
edge (sword)	*dhār*
either	*khwāh...khwāh* / *yā...yā*
elegant	*khush-numā*
elephant	*hāthī*
eloquent	*faṣīḥ*
embark	*nāo par charhnā*
embrace	*baghal-gīrī*
embroidery	*chikan-dozī*
emperor	*ḳaiṣar*
employ, *v.*	*naukar rakhnā*
employment	*kām, naukarī*
empty, *v.*	*khālī karnā*
end	*ākhir*
endeavour	*koshish*
endless	*be-ḥadd*
enemy	*dushman*
energy	*ḳuwwat*
engage, *v.*	*kām denā*
England	*inglistān*
English	*angrezī*
,, language	*angrezī zabān*
Englishman (I am an)	*main angrezī ādmī hūn*
enough	*bas*
,, (it is)	*yih bas hai*
enquire	*pūchhnā*
enter, *v.*	*andar ānā*
entirely	*bilkull*
envy, *s.*	*ḥasad karnā*
equal	*barābar*
error	*ghalaṭī, chūk*
escape, *s.*	*chhuṭkārā*
especially	*khuṣūṣan*
establish	*ḳā'im karnā*
eternal	*azalī, abadī*
Europe	*wilāyat*
European	*wilāyatī*
even, *ad.*	*bhī*

English.	Hindūstani.
event	*mājarā*
ever (always)	*hamesha*
every	*har ek*
evidence	*gawāhī*
evil	*badī, kharābī*
examine, *v.*	*taḥḳīk karnā*
examination	*imtiḥān*
example	*miṣāl*
,, (for)	*maṣālan*
except	*siwāe*
excessive	*nihāyat*
exchange, *v.*	*badal karnā*
exchange, *s.*	*badal*
excuse	*'uẕr*
excusable	*'uẕr ke ḳābil*
expense	*kharch*
experience	*tajriba*
experiment	*āzmā'ish*
explain	*samjhānā*
extinguish	*bujhā denā*
extract (strip)	*nikāl lenā*
extraordinary	*'ajīb*
extremely	*nihāyat*
eye-ball	*putlī*
eye-lash	*palak*
Faith	*īmān*
faithful	*īmāndār*
fall, *v.*	*gir paṛnā*
false (not true)	*jhūṭhā*
fame	*nek-nāmī*
famine	*ḳaḥt, kāl*
fan	*pankhā*
far	*dūr*
far from this? (how)	*yahān se kitnī dūr?*
farewell	*khudā ḥāfiẓ*
fast month (abstinence)	*roza kā mahīnā*

English.	Hindûstani.	English.	Hindûstani
fast (firm)	*maẕbūt*	flag	*nishān*
,, (quick)	*jald*	flat	*chapṭā*
,, (relig.)	*roza*	fleet	*tez-rau*
fat	*moṭā, farbih*	flesh	*gosht*
fate	*ḳismat*	flint	*patthar*
father	*bāp, wālid*	float, *v.*	*pānī par bahnā*
fatigue	*māndagī*	flock (herd)	*galla*
fault	*ḳuṣūr*	flog, *v.*	*mārnā*
,, (it is not my)	*yih merī taḳṣīr nahīṇ*	flour	*āṭā*
		flower, *s.*	*phūl*
favour	*mihrbānī*	,, garden	*phūlwāṛī*
fear, *s.*	*ḍar*	,, pot	*gul-dān*
fear, *v.*	*ḍarnā*	flute	*bānsrī*
feast	*ẕiyāfat*	fly, *v.*	*uṛnā*
feather	*par*	,, *s.*	*makkhī*
feed, *v.*	*khilānā*	foam	*phen*
feel, *v.*	*ṟikḳat rakhnā*	fog	*kuhāsā*
female (a)	*'aurat*	follow, *v.*	*pīchhe ānā*
ferry	*guẕr-ghāṭ*	food	*khwurāk*
ferryman	*ghāṭ-mānjī*	fool	*aḥmaḳ*
fertile	*zarkhez*	foolish	*be-wuḳūf*
festival	*teohār, 'īd*	for	*iske wāsṭe*
fever	*tap*	forage	*chārā*
few	*chand*	forbid, *v.*	*man' karnā*
fidelity	*wafādārī*	forehead	*peshānī*
field	*khet*	foreign	*pardes*
fig	*anjīr*	foreigner (a)	*pardesī*
fight, *v.*	*laṛnā*	forest	*jangal*
,, *s.*	*laṛā'ī*	forget, *v.*	*bhūl jānā*
fill, *v.*	*bharnā*	forgive, *v.*	*mu'āf karnā*
filthy	*mailā*	form	*shakl*
final	*ākhir*	formerly	*pahle se*
find, *v.*	*milnā*	forsake	*chhoṛ denā*
fine (delicate)	*bārīk, nāzuk*	fortress	*ḳil'a, burj*
finish	*tamām karnā*	fortunate	*khush-naṣīb*
finished (it is)	*yih ho chukā*	fortune	*māl*
fire	*āg*	forward	*āge*
firm	*sakht*	fountain	*chashma*
fisherman	*māhīgīr*	France	*farāns des*
fix	*lagānā*	fraud	*fareb*

English.	Hindûstânî.	English.	Hindûstânî.
free	*āzād*	go slowly	*āhiste chalo*
freedom	*āzādagī*	,, thou	*jāo*
Frenchman	*farāns des kā*	goat	*bakrā*
frequently	*akṣar* [*ādmī*	good	*achchhā* [*nā*
fresh (cool)	*ṭhanḍhā*	govern	*bādshāhat kar-*
friend	*dost*	government	*'amaldārī*
friendly	*dostī se*	governor	*ḥākim*
friendship	*dostī*	grain	*anāj, dāna*
fright, *s.*	*ḍar*	granary	*golā*
frog	*menḍak*	grandfather	*dādā*
from	*se*	grandmother	*dādī*
front	*āge*	granddaugh-	*potrī*
fruit	*mewā, phal*	grapes [ter	*angūr*
full (filled)	*bharā*	grass	*ghās*
furious	*ghuṣṣe se*	grateful	*iḥsānmand*
future	*āyanda*	gratis	*muft*
Gain, *v.*	*fā'ida uṭhānā*	grave, *s.*	*ḳabr*
gamble	*jū'ā khelnā*	graze	*charnā*
game	*khel*	great	*baṛā*
,, (chase)	*shikār*	grief	*ghamm, dukh*
gardener	*mālī*	grind, *v.*	*pīsnā*
garland	*phūloṇ kī mālā*	groom	*sā'is*
garlic	*lahsan*	ground	*zamīn*
gate	*phāṭak*	grow, *v.* [nel)	*ugnā*
gay	*khurram, khush*	guard (senti-	*pahra-wālā*
general	*'āmm*	guess, *v.*	*ḳiyās karnā*
generally	*akṣar*	guide, *v.*	*rāh batlānā*
generous	*sakhī*	,, (runner)	*rāh-numā*
gentle	*aṣīl*	gum	*gond*
gentleman	*ṣāḥib*	Habit	*dastūr, 'ādat*
gift	*in'ām*	(custom)	
give, *v.*	*denā*	,, (dress)	*poshāk*
glad	*khush*	hail	*olā*
glass	*kānch*	hall	*dālān*
,, (a)	*shīsha*	ham	*sū'ar kā gosht*
glory	*jalāl*	hammer	*mārtaul, haṭorā*
glue	*saresh*	handful	*muṭṭhī-bhar*
gnat	*machhar*	handsome	*khūbṣūrat*
go fast	*jaldī jāo*	hang (up)	*laṭkānā*
,, on	*chalo*	,, (execute)	*phāṇsī denā*

English.	Hindūstānī.	English.	Hindūstānī.
happen	*ho jānā*	honour	*'izzat*
happy	*k͟hush-dil*	hook	*ānkṛī*
hard	*sak͟ht*	hope, *v.*	*ummed rakhnā*
hare	*k͟har-gosh*	horn	*sing*
harem	*ḥaram*	horseman	*sawār*
harness	*sāz*	horse-shoe	*na'l*
harvest, *s.*	*faṣl*	hospitality	*mihmān-dārī*
hasten, *v.*	*jaldī karnā*	host	*mihmān-dār*
hastily	*jaldī se*	hot weather	*garmī kā mau-*
hate, *v.*	*'adāwat rakhnā*	how	*kaisā?* [*sim*
hawk	*bāz*	,, much?	*kitnā?*
he	*yih, wuh*	human	*insānī*
heal	*achchhā karnā*	hunger, *s.*	*bhūkh*
health	*mizāj, ṣiḥḥat*	hungry	*bhūkhā*
heap, *s.*	*ḍher*	hunt, *v.*	*shikār karnā*
hear	*sunnā*	hunter	*shikārī*
heat	*garmī*	hunting	*shikār karne ko*
heavy	*bhārī*		
heel, *s.*	*eṛī*	Ice	*barf*
height	*ūnchā'ī, bulan-*	idea	*k͟hayāl*
heir	*wāriṣ* [*dī*	idle	*sust*
help, *v.*	*madad denā*	if	*agar, jo*
,, *s.*	*madad*	ignorant	*nā-dān*
hemp	*san*	ill (sick)	*bīmār*
herd	*galla*	image	*putlā, but*
here	*yahāṇ*	imagination	*k͟hayāl*
here and there	*idhar udhar*	imitate	*naḳl karnā*
		immediately	*fauran*
hide, *v.*	*chhipānā*	immortal	*abadī*
,, *s.*	*chamṛā*	impatience	*be-ṣabr*
hideous	*bad-ṣūrat*	impertinence	*gustāk͟hī*
high	*ūnchā*	important	*ẓarūrī*
hill	*pahāṛ*	impossible	*nā-mumkin*
history	*tārīk͟h*	imprison	*ḳaid meṇ ḍālnā*
hold, *v.*	*pakaṛnā*	improper	*nā-munāsib*
hole	*chhed*	imprudent	*be-iḥtiyāṭ*
hollow	*mujauwaf*	in	*meṇ, andar*
holy	*muṣallī, ḳuddūs*	increase, *v.*	*baṛhānā, ziyāda karnā*
honest	*rāst-bāz*		
honey	*shahd*	indeed	*fil-wāḳi'*

English.	Hindūstanī.
India	*hind*
Indian (an)	*hindūstānī*
indigo	*nīl*
individual	*ādmī, shakhṣ*
indolent	*sust*
industrious	*miḥnatī*
inferior	*chhoṭā*
infidel	*kāfir*
infinite	*be-intihā*
inn	*musāfir-khāna*
innocent	*be-gunāh*
inquire, *v.*	*pūchhnā*
inquiry	*daryāft*
insane	*dīwāna, paglā*
inscription	*katba*
insensible	*be-hosh*
insolent	*gustākh*
inspector	*muhtamim*
instant (this)	*ek dam*
instant	*laḥẓa*
instead of	*'iwaẓ meṇ*
instinct	*samajh*
instrument	*āla, hathiyār*
insult	*be-'izzatī*
insurrection	*baghāwat*
intelligent	*hoshyār*
intention	*ḳaṣd*
interest	*sūd*
interpret, *v.*	*tashrīḥ karnā*
interpreter	*mutarjim*
invent	*ījād karnā*
invention	*ījād*
invisible	*ghā'ib*
irrigate, *v.*	*ābpāshī karnā*
it	*yih, wuh*
ivory	*hāthī-dānt*
Jacket	*kurta*
jail	*ḳaid-khāna*
jar	*ṭharā*

English.	Hindūstanī.
jealous	*ghayūr*
jealousy	*ghairat*
jelly	*jelī*
jest	*thaṭṭhā*
jester	*ṭhaṭhol*
jew	*yahūdī*
jewel	*jauhar*
join, *v.*	*joṛnā*
joint	*joṛ*
Jordan	*yārdan naddī*
journey	*safar*
joy	*khushī*
judge, *v.*	*faiṣala karnā*
,, *s.*	*ḥākim, jaj-ṣāḥib*
judicial	*'adālatī*
juggler	*jādūgar*
jump	*kūd*
just (equitable)	*'ādil*
justice	*inṣāf*
Keep, *v.*	*rakhnā*
kernel	*maghz, gūdā*
kettle	*keṭlī*
kick, *v.*	*lāt mārnā*
kid	*bakrī kā bachcha*
kill	*mār ḍālnā*
kind, *ad.*	*mihrbān*
,, *s.* (sort)	*ḳism*
king	*rājā*
kingdom (empire)	*bādshāhat*
kiss, *v.*	*bosa denā*
,, *s.*	*bosa*
kitchen	*bāwarchī-khāna*
knave	*daghābāz*
knot	*gānṭh, girah*
know (I do not)	*maiṇ nahīṇ jāntā hūṇ*

English.	Hindûstani.
Labour	*miḥnat*
lace	*les*
ladder	*sīṛhī*
lady	*ṣāḥiba*
lake	*tāl, talā'o*
lamb	*bheṛī kā bachcha*
lame	*langṛā*
lancet	*nashtar*
land, *v.*	*utarnā*
language	*zabān, bolī*
lantern	*lālṭain*
large	*baṛā*
last (the)	*sab se pichhlā*
late	*der meṇ*
laugh	*hansnā*
law	*ḳānūn, ā'īn*
lawful	*jā'iz*
lawyer	*wakīl*
lazy	*sust*
,, (to be) *v.*	*sust honā*
lead (guide)	*āge chalnā*
leaf (tree)	*pattā*
,, (book)	*waraḳ*
lean	*dublā, patlā*
,, against(to)	*ṭeknā*
learn	*sīkhnā*
leather	*chamṛā*
leave, *v.*	*chhoṛ denā, chhuṭṭī lenā*
leave, *s.*	*rukhṣat*
leech	*joṇk*
left	*bāḳī*
,, hand	*bāyāṇ*
,, (go to the)	*bā'eṇ jāo*
leg	*pāṇw*
legal	*ḳānūnī*
leisure	*furṣat*
lemon	*nīmū, nimbū*
lend, *v.*	*udhār denā*
length	*lambā'ī*
leopard	*chītā*
leper	*koṛhī*
leprosy	*koṛh*
less	*kam*
let, *v.*	*denā*
letter(epistle)	*khaṭṭ*
,, (alphabet)	*ḥarf*
level	*barābar*
liar	*jhūṭhā, daroghgo*
liberty	*āzādī*
library	*kutub-khāna*
lie, *v.*	*leṭnā*
,, *s.*	*jhūṭh bāt*
lies (to tell)	*jhūṭh bolnā*
life	*jān*
lift	*uṭhānā*
light	*roshan*
,, *v.*	*jalā denā*
,, (weight)	*halkā*
lightning	*bijlī*
like (to be)	*ham-shakl*
line	*saṭar*
listen	*sunnā*
little	*chhoṭā*
live, *v.*	*jīnā*
liver	*jigar, kalejā*
lizard	*ṭikṭikī*
load, *v.*	*lādnā*
,, (a gun)	*bandūḳ bharnā*
lock, *s.*	*ḳufl, tālā*
lock, *v.*	*ḳufl lagānā*
locust	*malakh, ṭiḍḍī*
long	*lambā*
look	*nazar*
loose, *ad.*	*ḍhīlā*
lord	*ṣāḥib, mālik, ḥuẓūr*
lose, *v.*	*khonā, hārnā*
loss	*nuḳṣān*
love, *s.*	*maḥabbat, pyār*

English.	Hindūstani.	English	Hindūstani.
love, *v.*	*pyār karnā*	memory	*yād*
lover	*'āshiḳ*	men	*mard, ādmī*
low	*nīchā*	mend	*marammat kar-*
luck	*ḳismat*	merchandise	*saudā, māl* [*nā*
lucky	*khush-naṣīb*	merchant	*saudāgar, bani-*
luggage	*māl, asbāb*	mercy	*raḥm* [*yā*
lungs	*shush, phephṛā*	merry	*khush*
		middle	*bīch*
Machine	*kal*	mill	*chakkī*
mad	*dīwāna*	mind	*'aḳl, hosh*
magazine	*kitāb*	mine (of me)	*merā*
magic	*jādū*	mirror	*ā'īna, darpan*
magistrate	*ḥākim* [*panāh*	mischief	*badī, nuḳṣān*
majesty	*ḥuẓūr, jahān-*	miser	*bakhīl*
make	*banānā, karnā*	miserable	*bechāra*
male	*nar*	misfortune	*muṣībat, āfat*
malice	*kīna*	mist	*kuhāsā*
man-of-war	*jangī jahāz*	mistake	*ghalaṭ*
manliness	*mardānagī*	mix, *v.*	*milānā*
manner	*ṭaraḥ*	model	*namūna*
many	*bahut*	modest	*sharmīlā*
many? (how)	*kitne?*	moist	*gīlā*
map	*naḳsha*	moment	*laḥẓa*
mare	*ghoṛī*	money	*paise, rūpīye*
mark	*dāgh, nishān*	,, (change)	*naḳd rūpīye*
marry, *v.*	*shādī karnā*	monkey	*bandar*
mast	*ḍol, mastūl*	more	*ziyāda*
master	*mālik*	morrow	*kal*
mat	*chaṭā'ī*	mortar	*okhlī*
meaning	*ma'nī, maṭlab*	,, (plaster)	*chūnā*
means (wealth)	*daulat*	mosque	*masjid*
measure	*māp*	moth	*parwāna*
,, *v.*	*māpnā*	move, *v.*	*hilnā*
medical man	*dākṭar, ḥakīm*	mount, *v.*	*chaṛhnā*
medicine	*dawā*	mountain	*pahāṛ*
meet, *s.*	*mulāḳāt*	mourn, *v.*	*ghamm karnā*
melon (water)	*kharbūza*	much	*bahut*
melt, *v.*	*galnā*	mud	*kīchaṛ*
memorandum	*yād-dāsht*	mule	*khachchar*
		murder	*khūn*

English.	Hindūstanī.
mushroom	chhātā
music	mūsīḳī
,, (the art)	rāg
musician	muṭrib
musk	mushk
musquito	machchhar
,, net	musahrī
must (you)	chāhiye
mutiny	balwā
my	merā
Nail (iron)	kīl, mekh
naked	nangā
name	nām
narrow	tang, sakṛā
nation	ḳaum
nature	khilḳat
,, (disposition)	ṭabī‘at, mizāj
near	nazdīk
necessary	ẓarūr
necessity	ẓarūrat
necklace	mālā
needle	sū'ī
neglect	ghaflat
negro	ḥabshī
neighbour	paṛosī
neither	na...na
nephew	bhatījā
nest	ghoṇslā
net	jāl
never	kabhī nahīṇ
nevertheless	tau bhī
new	nayā, tāza
news	khabar
next	dūsrā
night	rāt, shab
nightingale	‘andalīb
no	nahīṇ
noble	sharīf
nobleman	amīr
nobody	ko'ī nahīṇ
noise	āwāz, ghul
none	ko'ī nahīṇ
nonsense	behūda bāt
north	uttar, shamāl
not	na, nahīṇ
nothing	kuchh nahīṇ
notwithstanding	tau bhī
not yet	ab tak nahīṇ
nourish	pālnā
now (at present)	ab
number	‘adad
numerous	bahut
nurse	āyā
,, v.	dūdh pilānā; tīmārdārī karnā
nutmeg	jā'e-phal
Oar	ḍānḍ
oath	ḳasam
obedience	tābi‘dārī
obedient	ḥukm-bardār
obey, v.	mānnā
oblige, v.	mihrbānī karnā
obstinate	ẓiddī
obtain	milnā
occupation	dhandhā
often	akṣar
offence	taḳṣīr
office	daftar
officer (chief)	ḥākim
oil	tel
old	purānā
old (age)	būṛhāpā
old (man)	būṛhā
old (woman)	būṛhiyā
once	ek daf‘a
onion	piyāz

English.	Hindûstânî.	English.	Hindûstânî.
only	*khālī, fakat*	parrot	*totā*
open	*khulā*	part	*juz, ṭukṛā*
opinion	*khayāl, rā'e*	partner	*sharīk*
opium	*afyūn*	partridge	*tītar*
opportunity	*mauḳā'*	pass, *v.*	*guzar jānā*
oppose, *v.*	*sāmnā karnā*	passport	*parwāna*
opposite	*sāmne*	patience	*ṣabr*
or	*yā*	patient	*ṣābir*
orange	*nārangī*	pattern	*namūna*
order (arrangement)	*band-o-bast*	pay, *v.*	*adā karnā*
		payment	*adā*
order (command)	*ḥukm*	peace	*ṣulḥ*
		peacock	*mor*
order, *v.*	*ḥukm denā*	peasant	*ra'īyat*
oriental	*mashriḳī*	people	*log*
origin	*aṣl, bunyād*	perfume	*khush-bū*
ornament	*gahnā*	perhaps	*shāyad*
other	*aur ek*	perish, *v.*	*mar jānā*
out	*bāhar*	permission	*ijāzat*
oven	*tanūr*	permit, *v.*	*ijāzat denā*
over	*ūpar*	Persia	*Irān, Fārs*
overseer	*nāẓir*	Persian	*Irānī, Fārsī*
owe, *v.*	*ḳārẓ rakhnā*	person	*shakhṣ*
owl	*ullū*	perspiration	*pasīna*
own (possess)	*apnā*	petition	*'arẓ, guzārish*
ox	*bail*	pewter	*jast*
		philosopher	*ḥakīm*
Page (of a book)	*ṣafḥa*	pickaxe	*phauṛā*
		piece	*ṭukṛā*
page (in waiting)	*launḍā*	pilgrim	*jātrī*
		pill	*golī*
pain	*dard*	pillage	*lūṭ*
paint, *v.*	*rang lagānā*	pillar	*sitūn, khambā*
pair	*joṛā*	pin	*pīn*
palace	*maḥal*	pincers	*chimṭā*
palm-tree	*khajūr gāchh*	pipe (tube)	*nal*
pan	*tāba*	pipe (for narghile)	*pīpā*
pan (frying)	*farā'i pān*		
pardon	*mu'āf*	pipe (for tobacco)	*ḥuḳḳa*
pardon, *v.*	*mu'āf karnā*		

English.	Hindústáni.
pitch	*ķīr*
pity	*afsos, raḥm*
place	*jagah*
plain (even)	*barābar*
plant	*paudhā*
play, *v.*	*khelnā*
play (an instrument)	*bajānā*
pleasant	*achchhā, dil-pazīr*
plenty	*bahut*
plough	*hal*
plunder	*lūṭ*
poet	*shā'ir*
poetry	*shi'r*
point	*nok, nuḳta*
poison	*zahr*
police	*polīs*
politeness	*akhlāḳ*
pomegranate	*anār*
pond	*tālāb*
poor	*gharīb, kangāl*
poppy	*post*
pork	*sū'ar kā gosht*
porter (carrier)	*ķulī*
porter (door-keeper)	*darbān*
portmanteau	*peṭī*
possible	*mumkin*
post (for letters)	*ḍāk, ṭappāl*
post (house)	*ḍāk-ghar*
pot	*degchī*
pound	*ādhā ser*
pour, *v.*	*ḍāl denā*
poverty	*iflās*
power	*ķudrat*
powerful	*zorāwar*
praise	*ta'rīf*
praise, *v.*	*ta'rīf karnā*

English.	Hindústáni.
pray, *v.*	*namāz paṛhnā*
prayer	*namāz*
prefer	*pasand karnā*
present, *ad.*	*ḥāẓir*
present (gift)	*in'ām*
pretty	*suthrā*
prey	*shikār*
price	*ķīmat, dām*
pride	*ghurūr*
priest	*imām*
prince	*shāh-zāda*
prince (royal)	*rāj-kumār*
princess	*shāh-zādī*
private	*khāṣṣ*
privy	*pai-khāna*
probably	*shāyad, ghāliban*
procession	*sawārī*
proclamation	*ishtihār, manādī*
produce, *v.*	*paidākarnā*
profit	*fā'ida, nafa'*
promise, *v.*	*wa'da karnā*
proof	*dalīl*
proper	*durust, ṭhīk*
prophet	*paighambar*
protect	*bachānā*
proud	*maghrūr*
province	*ṣūbah*
provision	*tosha*
prudence	*khabar-dārī*
prudent	*khabar-dār*
publish, *v.*	*jārī karnā*
pull, *v.*	*khīnchnā*
pump	*bam*
punish	*sazā denā*
pupil	*shāgird*
pure	*ṣāf*
purposely	*irāde se*
purse	*thailī*
push	*dhakkā*
put, *v.*	*rakh denā*

English.	Hindūstanī.
put out	nikāl denā
Quadruped	chaupāya
quail	bater
quantity	miḳdār
quarrel	jhagṛā
quarter ($\frac{1}{4}$th)	chauthā'ī, pā'o
quarter (in battle)	amān
quarter (of a town)	maḥalla
queen	rānī, malika
question	sawāl
quick (agile)	jald, tez
quite	bi-l-kul
Radish	mūlī
rag	gudaṛ
railway train	rel-gāṛī
rainy	pānī kā
raise, v.	uṭhānā, khaṛā karnā
raisin	kishmish
rank	'uhda
rapid	jald, tez
rare	nādir
rascal	bad-ma'āsh
rash	be-lihāẓ
raw	kachchā
ray	kiran
razor	usturā
read	paṛhnā
ready	taiyār
real	ḥaḳīḳī
rear	pīchhe
reason	sabab
receipt	rasīd
receive, v.	milnā
recently	in dinoṇ meṇ
recollect	yād karnā
recompense	ajr
record	likhnā

English.	Hindūstanī.
recover (illness)	achchhā ho jānā
reed	nā'e
reflection	soch
refresh one's self	tāzagī ḥāṣil honā
refuse	ā<u>kh</u>or, fuẓla
region	mulk
regulations	ā'īn, ḳānūn
rejoice, v.	<u>kh</u>ush honā
relation (family)	sagā
release	chhoṛ denā
relieve	ārām denā
religion	dīn, ma<u>z</u>hab
remain	ṭhaharnā
remedy	'ilāj
remember, v.	yād karnā
remind	yād dilānā
remove, v.	le-jānā, nikāl denā
rent (hire)	kirāya
rent (tear)	phāṛ, chīr
repair	marammat karnā
repeat	phir bolnā
report	<u>kh</u>abar
reproach	ṭa'na, malāmat
repulse, v.	shikast denā
request	dar<u>kh</u>wāst
resign	chhoṛ denā
resist	muzāḥamat
respect	adab
rest	ārām
rest, v.	ārām karnā
retreat	<u>kh</u>alwat-gāh
return (come back)	phir ānā, wāpas ānā
revenge	intiḳām
reward	in'ām, ba<u>kh</u>shish
rheumatism	bā'ī
rib	panjar, paslī
ribbon	fītah

English.	Hindûstani.	English.	Hindûstani.
rice	*dhān*	sale [tion)	*farokht*
rich	*daulat-mand*	sale (by auc-	*nīlām*
ride, *v.*	*sawārī-karnā*	saltpetre	*shorā*
rider	*sawār*	salvation	*najāt*
rifle	*bandūḳ*	salve	*marham*
right (not left)	*dāhinā*	same	*ek-hī, wuhī*
right (just	*wājib*	sample	*namūna*
claim)		sand	*ret, bālū*
right (hand)	*dāhine*	savage, *ad.*	*janglī*
right, *s.*	*ṭhīk*	save, *v.*	*bachānā*
ring	*angūṭhī*	say; I say	*bolnā ; maiṇ*
ripe	*pakkā, pukhta*	[you)	*boltā hūṇ*
rise, *v.*	*uṭhnā, uṭh jānā*	say? (what do	*kyā bolte ho ?*
road	*rāstā*	scale (bal-	*tarāzū*
roast	*kabāb*	ance)	
rob	*lūṭnā*	scarce	*kamyāb*
robber	*ḍakait*	scarcely	*kamyābī se*
robbery	*ḍakaitī*	scarcity	*ḳillat*
rock	*patthar, sang*	scarlet	*lāl*
roof	*chhappar*	scatter, *v.*	*chhitrānā*
root	*jaṛ*	scholar	*shāgird*
rope	*rassī, ḍorī*	school	*maktab*
rose	*gul*	schoolmaster	*ustād*
rosewater	*gul-āb*	science	*'ilm*
rot	*saṛnā*	scorpion	*bichchhū*
rotten	*saṛā*	search	*talāsh, ḍhunḍh*
rough	*kharkharā*	secret	*bhed, rāz*
round	*gol*	sect	*firḳa*
rub	*ragaṛnā*	see, *v.*	*dekhnā*
,, together	*mālish karnā*	seed	*biyā, bīj*
ruby	*yāḳūt*	seek	*ḍhūnḍhnā*
rude	*gustākh*	seldom	*kam*
ruin	*kharābī*	self (myself)	*apnā*
run, *v.*	*dauṛnā*	sell (to)	*bechnā*
rust	*zang*	send, *v.*	*bhejnā*
		sentence	*jumla*
Said	*bolā*	sense	*'aḳl*
safe	*sālim*	separate, *v.*	*judā karnā*
sagacity	*'aḳl, hosh*	serpent	*sāmp, nāg*
salary	*tankhwāh, ṭalab*	servant	*naukar*

English	Hindūstanī.	English.	Hindūstanī.
serve, *v.*	*khidmat karnā*	station (rank)	*martaba*
service	*khidmat*	steady	*ḳā'im*
settlement	*band-o-bast*	steal, *v.*	*chorī karnā*
several	*chand*	steam	*bhāph*
severe	*sakht*	step	*ḳadam*
sew, *v.*	*sīnā, silā'ī kar-*	still	*chup*
shade	*sāya* [*nā*	sting, *s.*	*ḍank*
shake, *v.*	*hilānā*	stock (capital)	*pūnjī*
shame	*sharm*	stop, *v.*	*kharā rahnā,*
shape	*shakl*		*roknā*
sharpen	*tez karnā*	storm	*ṭūfān*
shave, *v.*	*ḥajāmat karnā*	story	*ḳiṣṣa, kahānī*
she	*yih, wuh*	straight	*sīdhā*
sheath	*miyān*	stranger	*ghair ādmī*
shed, *v.*	*phailnā*	straw	*bichālī*
shield	*ḍhāl*	strength	*zor*
shine	*chamaknā*	strong	*ḳawī*
ship	*jahāz*	,, (solid)	*maẓbūṭ*
shoe (horse)	*na'l*	stupid	*be-wuḳūf*
shoot, *v.*	*bandūḳ chalānā*	stupid (inex-	*nā-wāḳif*
shop	*dūkān*	perienced)	
shopkeeper	*dūkān-dār*	success	*kāmyābī*
shore	*kināra*	sudden	*achānak*
short	*kotāh, chhoṭā*	suffer, *v.*	*bardāsht karnā*
show, *v.*	*dikhlānā*	sufficient	*bas, kāfī*
shut, *v.*	*band karnā*	sugar candy	*miṣrī*
shut the door	*darwāza band*	sulphur	*gandhak*
sick	*bīmār* [*karo*	summit	*choṭī*
sickness	*bīmārī*	superfluous	*fuẓūl*
side	*ṭaraf, bāzū*	support, *v.*	*āsrā denā*
sieve	*ghirbāl*	surgeon	*jarrāḥ*
sight	*naẓar*	surprise	*ta'ajjub*
sign	*ishāra, nishān*	suspicion	*gumān*
square (a)	*chauk*	swear	*ḳasam khānā*
stable, *adj.*	*maẓbuṭ*	sweep, *v.*	*jhāṛnā*
stand, *v.*	*kharā rahnā*	sweet	*mīṭhā*
star	*tārā, sitāra*	sweetmeats	*miṭhā'ī*
starch	*kānjī*	swell, *v.*	*sūjnā*
start, *v.*	*chaunknā*	swift	*tez-rau*
station	*chaukī*	swim, *v.*	*pairnā*

English.	Hindūstānī.	English.	Hindūstānī.
Take, *v.*	*lenā*	throw, *v.*	*pheṇknā*
take care	*khabardār honā*	tie, *v.*	*bāndhnā*
talk, *v.*	*bātchīt karnā*	tight	*tang*
tall	*lambā*	tile	*khaprā*
tank	*talā'o*	till, *v.*	*khetī karnā*
taste	*maza*	tired	*thakā*
taste, *v.*	*chakhnā*	to	*ko*
tax	*maḥṣūl*	toast, *v.*	*seṇknā*
,, (land)	*zamīn-ṭikas*	(bread)	
teach, *v.*	*sikhānā*	tobacco	*tambākū*
teacher (of	*munshī*	together	*sāth*
languages)		tomb	*ḳabr*
telescope	*dūr-bīn*	tongue (hold	*chup raho*
tell, *v.*	*kahnā*	your)	
temper	*mizāj, ṭabī'at*	too	*bhī*
temperate	*mu'tadil*	tools	*hathiyār*
	parhezgār	top	*choṭī*
temple	*masjid*	torch	*mash'al*
tent	*khīma, tambū,*	torment	*'azāb*
	ḍerā	tortoise	*kachhū'ā*
terrible	*khauf-nāk*	touch, *v.*	*chhūnā*
thank	*shukr*	towards	*kī ṭaraf*
thank, *v.*	*shukr karnā*	traitor	*namak-ḥarām*
thankful	*shukr-guzār*		*daghābāz*
then	*tab*	translate, *v.*	*tarjuma karnā*
there	*wahāṇ*	translation	*tarjuma*
they	*ye, we*	translator	*mutarjim*
thick	*moṭā*	travel, *v.*	*safar karnā*
thief	*chor*	traveller	*musāfir*
thigh	*jāngh*	,, European	*gorā musāfir*
thin	*patlā*	treachery	*daghābāzī*
thing	*chīz* [*karnā*	treasure	*khazāna*
think, *v.*	*sochnā, khayāl*	tremble, *v.*	*kāmpnā*
thirsty	*piyāsā*	tribe	*ḳaum*
thorn	*kāṇṭā*	trouble	*taklīf*
those	*wuh*	true	*sach, ṣādiḳ*
thou	*tū*	trunk (box)	*ṣandūḳ*
thought	*soch, dhyān*	trust, *v.*	*i'timād rakhnā*
thread	*sūt, tāgā*	trustee	*mu'tamad*
threaten, *v.*	*dhamkānā*	truth	*sach bāt*

English.	Hindûstânî.
try, *v.* (endeavour)	*koshish karnā*
try (prove)	*jāṇchnā*
tune	*tān*
turban	*pagṛī*
twist, *v.*	*aiṇṭhnā*
tyrant	*ẓālim*
Ugly	*bad-ṣūrat*
under	*nīche*
understand	*samajhnā*
,, ? (do you)	*samajhte ho?*
unfortunate	*kam-bak͟ht*
unjust	*be-inṣāf*
until	*jab tak...nahīṇ*
upon	*par*
uproar	*g͟hul*
us	*ham*
,, (to us)	*ham ko*
use	*kām*
,, (it is of no)	*yih kuchh kām kā nahīṇ*
useful	*kām kā*
useless	*kuchh kām kā nahīṇ*
usual	*ma'mūlī*
Vagabond	*luchchā, bad-zāt*
vain	*dimāg͟hī*
valuable	*ḳīmatī*
value, *n.*	*ḳīmat*
,, *v.*	*ḳadr karnā*
various	*chand ḳism kā*
vast	*baṛā*
vegetables	*tarkārī, sabzī*
veil	*niḳāb*
vein	*nas, rag*
velvet	*mak͟hmal*
verse (poetry)	*chhand*
very	*nihāyat*

English.	Hindûstânî.
vile	*k͟harāb*
vineyard	*angūristān*
violence	*zor, jabr*
virgin	*bākira*
virtue	*k͟hūbī*
virtuous (honourable)	*'izzat-dār*
visible	*ẓāhir, naẓar meṇ*
visit	*mulāḳāt*
voice	*āwāz*
vomit, *v.*	*ubkā'ī karnā*
vulgar	*kamīna*
vulture	*gidh*
Wager	*sharṭ*
wages	*ujrat*
waist	*kamar*
wait, *v.*	*ṣabr karnā*
waiter	*k͟hidmatgār, ḥāẓir-bāsh*
wake, *v.*	*jagānā*
walk, *v.*	*sair karnā, hawā khānā*
wall	*dīwār*
wander, *v.*	*bhaṭaknā*
want, *v.*	*chāhnā*
war	*laṛā'ī*
warm	*garm*
wash, *v.*	*dhonā*
washer-woman	*dhobin*
wasp	*birnī*
waste, *v.*	*k͟harāb karnā*
watch (time-piece)	*ghaṛī*
watch (milit.)	*pahre-wālā*
,, *v.*	*ḥifāẓat karnā*
watchman	*chaukī-dār*
water-carrier	*bihishtī*
water-melon	*tarbūz*

English.	Hindūstānī.	English.	Hindūstānī.
wave	*mauj*	wire	*tār*
wax	*mom*	wisdom	*'aḳl*
way (road)	*rāh, rāstā*	wise	*'aḳlmand*
we	*ham*	wish, *v.*	*chāhnā*
weak	*kam-zor*	wish, *s.*	*khwāhish*
wealth	*dhan, daulat*	with	*ke sāth*
weary	*thakā*	within [side)	*andar*
weather	*mausim*	without (out-	*bāhar*
weave	*binnā*	withoutdoubt	*be-shak, ẓarūr*
wedding	*shādī, byāh*	witness	*shāhid, gawāh*
weep, *v.*	*ronā*	wolf	*bheṛiyā*
weigh, *v.*	*tolnā*	wonderful	*'ajīb*
weight	*wazn*	wood (forest)	*jangal*
welcome (a)	*mubārak*	wood(timber)	*lakṛī*
well (good)	*achchhā*	wool	*ūn, pashm*
,, (a water)	*kū'āṇ*	woollen	*pashm kā*
west	*pachchham*	word	*bāt*
wet	*bhīgā, gīlā*	work	*kām*
what [say?	*kyā!*	worm	*kīṛā*
what do you	*kyā kahte ho?*	worth (to be)	*lā'iḳ honā*
wheat	*gehūṇ*	worthy	*lā'iḳ*
wheel	*pahiyā*	wound, *v.*	*zakhm denā*
when	*kab?*	write, *v.*	*likhnā*
whence	*kahāṇ se*	writer	*kātib*
where	*kahāṇ*	,, (copyist)	*naḳl-navīs*
which? *inter.*	*kaun*	writing	*lekhā*
whip	*chābuk*	wrong	*nā-durust*
whirlwind	*gird-bād*	Yard (court)	*ṣaḥn*
whistle, *v.*	*sīṭī bajānā*	,, (measure)	*gaz*
who (*rel.*)	*jo, jaun*	yes	*hāṇ, jī hāṇ*
who? (*inter.*)	*kaun?*	yet	*lekin*
whole	*tamām*	yet (not)	*ab tak*
whose?	*kis kā?*	yoke	*jū'ā*
why?	*kyūṇ?*	you	*tum*
wide	*chauṛā*	young	*jawān*
widow	*bewā*	your	*tumhārā*
wild	*janglī*	youth	*jawānī*
win, *v.*	*jītnā*	Zeal	*tapāk, josh*
wings	*par*	zealous	*sargarm*
wipe, *v.*	*poṇchh denā*	zephyr	*bād-i-ṣabā.*

MEMORANDA

MEMORANDA

MEMORANDA

MEMORANDA

MEMORANDA

MEMORANDA